Dubai
An Aerial Tour

Dubai
An Aerial Tour

Dirk Laubner

MOTIVATE
PUBLISHING

Published by Motivate Publishing

Dubai: PO Box 2331, Dubai, UAE
Tel: (+971 4) 282 4060; fax: (+971 4) 282 0428
e-mail: books@motivate.ae   www.booksarabia.com

Office 508, Building No 8, Dubai Media City, Dubai, UAE
Tel: (+971 4) 390 3550; fax: (+971 4) 390 4845

Abu Dhabi: PO Box 43072, Abu Dhabi, UAE
Tel: (+971 2) 677 2005; fax: (+971 2) 677 0124

London: Acre House, 11/15 William Road, London NW1 3ER
e-mail: motivateuk@motivate.ae

Directors: Obaid Humaid Al Tayer and Ian Fairservice

Original Text: Pippa Sanderson

Consultant Editor: David Steele
Deputy Editor: Moushumi Nandy
Assistant Editor: Zelda Pinto
Art Director: Andrea Willmore
Senior Designer: Cithadel Francisco
General Manager Books: Jonathan Griffiths

Additional Photography: Motivate Publishing 113,119,125

© Translations 2006: Yves Le Scieller and Catherine Demangeot (French);
Frank Schleper (German); Valery Nikonorov (Russian)

© Motivate Publishing and Dirk Laubner 2007

First Printed 2007
Reprinted 2007, 2008

ISBN: 978 1 86063 208 2

British Library Cataloguing-in-Publication Data. A catalogue record for this book
is available from the British Library.

Printed by Rashid Printers and Stationers LLC, Ajman, UAE

Front cover:

In the red sand dunes on the road to Hatta, tourists enjoy off-roading in 4x4.
In den roten Sanddünen an der Landstraße nach Hatta genießen Besucher
eine Offroad-Tour im Geländewagen.
Des touristes goûtent les plaisirs du 4x4 sur les dunes de sable rouge de la
route menant à Hatta.
Среди дюн из красного песка, лежащих на пути в Хатту, туристы
получают удовольствие от езды по бездорожью на «4x4».
عربي يتمتع السياح بمزايا قيادة سيارات الدفع الرباعي خلال عبورهم كثبان الرمال الحمراء في طريقهم إلى حتّا.

Back cover:

The Al Safa Interchange was redesigned to ease Dubai's traffic congestion.
Die Al Safa Interchange wurde umgestaltet, um Dubais steigendem
Verkehrsaufkommen gewachsen zu sein.
L'échangeur Al Safa a été refait pour essayer d'alléger les problèmes de
circulation de Dubaï.
Дорожная развязка в Аль Сафе была модернизирована, чтобы
уменьшить пробки на дорогах.
عربي أعيد تصميم تقاطع الصفا لتخفيف الاحتقان المروري في دبي.

Half-title page:

A traditional racing dhow.
Ein traditionelles Renn-Dhau.
Un boutre de course traditionnel.
Традиционное быстроходное доу.
عربي سفينة بوم شراعية تقليدية تستخدم في سباقات السفن الشراعية.

Title page:

Madinat Jumeirah, a recreation of ancient Arabia.
Madinat Jumeirah, inspiriert durch das Alte Arabien.
Le Madinat Jumeirah, une recréation de l'ancienne Arabie.
Мадинат Джумейра воссоздание старинной Аравии.
عربي تعيد مدينة جميرا إحياء تراث المدن العربية القديمة.

Imprint page:

Construction of luxury villas on the Palm Jumeirah.
Bau von Luxusvillen auf The Palm Jumeirah.
Construction de villas de luxe sur le Palm Jumeirah.
Строительство роскошных вилл на Палм Джумейре.
عربي مشروع لبناء فلل فخمة في جزيرة نخلة جميرا.

Introduction

Dubai is an emirate of fascinating contrasts. On the one hand is the beauty of the desert dunes, taking on poetic hues at dawn and, on the other, the 21st-century skyscrapers overlooking the city's highways. Although Dubai is an ultra-modern metropolis, it remains steeped in heritage. *Dubai - An Aerial Tour* guides the reader through this amazing landscape of life and colour, a landscape that combines the old-world charm of the souks with the modern-day grandeur of hi-tech shopping malls.

Dirk Laubner captures the essence of this breathtaking emirate with his brilliant aerial photography. Ranging from a bird's-eye view of the

modern Arabian architecture of Madinat Jumeirah, and the bustling banks of the Creek that embody the city's trading traditions, to the majestic dunes and mountains, his camera has recorded it all.

Dubai - An Aerial Tour is a photographer's unique celebration of the city's modern architecture, alluring landscapes and natural heritage. The brilliant photography captures the spirit of the city from the air while providing an amazing new perspective on a familiar landscape.

Acknowledgements: I'd like to thank the people of Dubai, who were always friendly and willing to lend a hand and share their ideas towards the photography for this book. I'd especially like to thank Capt Khalid Masud Butt from the Umm al-Qaiwain Aeroclub and Capt Hank Harrington from Heli Dubai, along with Capt Neils Heibrock from Dragon Air, who carried out essential homework for me; Nelson from Prolab; my partners at Motivate Publishing; Jessica Lindner, who took me round Dubai and always wore a smile; and my eight-year-old son, David, who gave me courage and patience, especially when a *shamal* threatened one particular flight and challenged the project.

قسم خور من مياه البحر المالحة دبي إلى شطرين هما ديرة وبر دبي. ولعب هذا الخور دوراً محورياً في ازدهار دبي التجاري، حيث شكل مرفأً طبيعياً محمياً من الأنواء البحرية، استخدمته السفن الشراعية في شحن شتى أنواع البضائع بين ساحلي الخليج العربي والإيراني وصولاً إلى الهند وسواحل أفريقيا الشرقية. ويشاهد في أعلى يسار الصورة، ميناء راشد المجاور لقرية التراث في منطقة الشندغة العريقة. وتجسد تلك القرية الحياة في عصر الغوص لاصطياد اللالئ والكثير من نمط الحياة التقليدي في دبي القديمة.

🇬🇧 Dubai is a city divided by a waterway, a saltwater inlet known as the Creek. The emirate's fortunes have been dependent on this crucial waterway since the first settlement was established on its banks centuries ago. It remains the main artery of the city and separates Bur Dubai on one side from Deira on the other. Near the mouth of the Creek, in the Shindagha district pictured at the top left of the photograph, the modern Port Rashid sits adjacent to a heritage village and the replica of an old pearl-diving village. These hug the shoreline and provide fascinating insights into Dubai's traditional culture.

🇫🇷 Dubaï est divisée en deux par une voie navigable, un bras de mer que l'on appelle la crique. Le destin de l'émirat a toujours été lié à cette voie navigable et ce depuis l'établissement des premières habitations sur ses rives, il y a de nombreux siècles. Elle demeure encore l'artère principale de la ville, séparant Bur Dubaï d'un côté, de Deira de l'autre. Près de son embouchure, dans le quartier de Shindagha, en haut à gauche, le très moderne Port Rashid se trouve situé à côté d'un village traditionnel et de la réplique d'un ancien village perlier. Ces villages bordent la crique et offrent un aperçu fascinant de la culture traditionnelle émirienne.

🇩🇪 Die Stadt Dubai wird von einem Meeresarm durchzogen, der Creek genannt wird. Seit der Zeit der ersten Besiedlung seiner Ufer vor Hunderten von Jahren hängt das Glück des Emirats von dieser wichtigen Wassserstraße ab. Sie trennt Bur Dubai auf der einen Seite von Deira auf der anderen und ist bis heute eine der Hauptarterien der Stadt. In der Nähe der Mündung, in der Nähe des Shindagha-Bezirks oben links im Foto, befindet sich der moderne Hafen Port Rashid neben den Museumsdörfern Heritage Village und Diving Village. Diese befinden sich direkt an der Küste und ermöglichen eine faszinierende Einsicht in die traditionelle Kultur Dubais.

🇷🇺 Дубай – это город, разделенный водным путем, узким морским заливом, известным под названием "Узкий Залив". Судьбы эмирата зависели от этого важного водного пути с того самого момента, когда на его берегах столетия назад появилось первое поселение. Он остается главной артерией города и отделяет Бур Дубай на одной стороне от Дейры на другой. Около устья Узкого Залива, в районе Шиндага (на фотографии вверху слева) расположен современный Порт Рашид, а по соседству с ним находятся "деревня исторического наследия" (воспроизводящая прежний для здешних мест образ жизни) и точная копия старинной деревни ныряльщиков за жемчугом. Они занимают береговую линию и позволяют совершить увлекательное проникновение в традиционную культуру Дубая.

يعتبر بيت الشيخ سعيد آل مكتوم الذي حكم دبي بين عامي ١٩١٢ و١٩٥٨، من أبرز المعالم التراثية في منطقة الشندغة. وقد تمت إعادة تأهيل البيت، المتميز ببراجيله الهوائية المرتفعة والذي يشاهد في الجانب الأيسر من أسفل الصورة بالقرب من موقع مسيّج للحفريات الأثرية، وتم تحويله إلى متحف للتراث المحلي. ويضم المتحف عدداً كبيراً من الأدوات والخرائط والصور التي تمثل دبي القديمة.

Also in Shindagha is the home of a former Ruler – Sheikh Saeed Al Maktoum – who ruled Dubai from 1912–1958. His home, with its prominent windtowers, can be seen at the bottom left of the photograph, next to a fenced-off area undergoing archaeological excavation. Sheikh Saeed House has been renovated and transformed into a museum containing many intriguing displays of photographs of old Dubai, maps and historical memorabilia.

In Shindagha steht auch die Residenz eines der ehemaligen Herrscher von Dubai, Scheich Saeed Al Maktoum (1912-1958). Der Bau mit seinen Windtürmen ist im Foto unten links zu sehen, neben einem eingezäunten Gebiet, auf dem archäologische Ausgrabungen stattfinden. Das Gebäude wurde renoviert und ist heute ein Museum mit vielen interessanten Ausstellungen von Fotos zu Dubais Geschichte, Landkarten und anderen historischen Objekten.

Dans ce même quartier de Shindagha se trouve aussi la demeure de l'ancien souverain – Cheikh Saeed Al Maktoum – qui a gouverné Dubaï entre 1912 et 1958. Sa demeure, dotée de tours à vent imposantes, est visible en bas à gauche, près d'un enclos où s'exécutent des fouilles archéologiques. La demeure de Cheikh Saeed a été rénovée et transformée en un musée où sont exposées de nombreuses photos du vieux Dubaï, des cartes et des pièces historiques.

В Шиндаге также находится жилище бывшего правителя – Шейха Саееда Аль Мактума, который правил в Дубае с 1912 по 1958 год. Его дом с двумя выступающими ветровыми башнями можно видеть в левом нижнем углу фотографии, около охранной зоны, где ведутся археологические раскопки. Дом Шейха Саееда был восстановлен и превращен в музей, в котором экспонируются многие увлекательные выставки фотографий старого Дубая, карт и исторических достопримечательностей.

تقع دبي على مفترق طرق التجارة العالمية بين آسيا وأوروبا، ويرجح الكثير من المؤرخين أن يكون خور دبي أحد أقدم المرافىء الطبيعية في العالم. ولا يزال بإمكان زائري دبي حتى اليوم، مشاهدة العديد من سفن البوم التقليدية راسية في الخور تحت ظلال ناطحات السحاب العملاقة المبنية من الفولاذ والخرسانة والزجاج. وتشاهد في أعلى يمين الصورة، جزيرة نخلة ديرة ومدينة دبي البحرية اللتان تعتبران من أضخم المشاريع العقارية الفائقة التطور والفخامة التي تقام في دبي حالياً، إضافة إلى المبنى الشامخ لفندق حياة ريجنسي.

🇬🇧 Dubai is at the global trading crossroads between Europe and Asia, and historians believe its Creek is probably one of the oldest ports in the world. Today, visitors can spy traditional dhows nestled in the shade of the most modern, state-of-the-art, glass-and-chrome buildings. Land reclamation for The Palm Deira and Dubai Maritime City can be seen at the top right of the photograph, and the tall structure standing on its own on the Corniche is The Hyatt.

🇫🇷 Dubaï se trouve au carrefour du marché mondial entre l'Europe et l'Asie. Les historiens pensent que la crique est l'un des plus anciens ports du monde. À présent, les visiteurs peuvent contempler des boutres traditionnels, blottis à l'ombre de bâtiments ultramodernes en verre et acier poli. On peut observer le déplacement de sable pour le Palm Deira et Dubai Maritime City en haut à droite de la photo. La haute structure isolée sur la Corniche est celle de l'hôtel Hyatt.

🇩🇪 In Dubai kreuzen sich die Handelsrouten zwischen Europa und Asien, und Historiker halten den Creek für einen der ältesten Häfen der Welt. Heute kann der Besucher die traditionellen Dhaus im Schatten der modernsten und technologisch ausgereiftesten Gebäude aus Glas und Chrom bewundern. Im Foto ist oben rechts auch die Neulandgewinnung für die Dubai Maritime City und für The Palm Deira zu sehen. Das alleinstehende hohe Gebäude an der Corniche ist das Hyatt Hotel.

🇷🇺 Дубай расположен на мировом торговом перекрестке между Европой и Азией, и историки считают, что на Узком Заливе, вероятно, находится один из самых древних портов в мире. Сегодня гости могут увидеть традиционные *доу*, укрытые в тени самых современных, построенных по последнему слову техники, зданий из стекла и хромированного металла. Мелиорацию земель для Палм Дейры и приморской части Дубая можно увидеть в правом верхнем углу фотографии, а высокое сооружение, отдельно стоящее на некотором возвышении, – это отель "Хайятт".

عربي تتميز مباني دبي بهندستها المعمارية الفائقة الحداثة والجمال والتطور، وتضم المئات من الأبراج السكنية والمكتبية والفندقية المبنية من الخرسانة والفولاذ والزجاج. ويشاهد في الصورة برجان تجاريان توأمان يتوسطان مجموعة من المباني العصرية مختلفة الارتفاع، ويطلان على ساحات لرصف السيارات وسفن بوم خشبية تقليدية راسية في خور دبي، بينما تنتشر في خلفية الصورة مئات المباني السكنية والمكتبية الحديثة والأقل ارتفاعاً، لتشكل لوحة بديعة تجمع بين مختلف مراحل التطور العمراني للمدينة.

🇬🇧 Dubai boasts exceptional architecture, with soaring chrome-and-glass skyscrapers, such as the Twin Towers. Here, they reflect the afternoon sun and mingle seamlessly with the large, traditional wooden dhows below them, providing a complementary blend of both ancient and modern Arabia.

▬ Dubai ist stolz auf seine außergewöhnliche Architektur mit in die Höhe ragenden Wolkenkratzern aus Chrom und Glas, wie beispielsweise den Twin Towers. Hier spiegeln sie die Nachmittagssonne wider und stellen zusammen mit den großen traditionellen Dhaus aus Holz zu ihren Füßen ein kontrastreiches Bild dar, in dem sich das klassische und das moderne Arabien mischen.

🇫🇷 Dubaï bénéficie d'une architecture exceptionnelle aux gratte-ciels d'acier et de verre, dont les Twin Towers. Elles reflètent ici le soleil de l'après-midi et s'intègrent admirablement avec les grands boutres traditionnels en bois à leurs pieds, formant une parfaite complémentarité entre l'Arabie ancienne et moderne.

▬ Дубай славится своей необыкновенной архитектурой – поднимающимися ввысь небоскребами из стекла и хромированного металла, такими как Башни-близнецы. Здесь они отражают послеполуденное солнце и неразличимо сливаются с большими традиционными деревянными суднами–доу под ними, придавая тем самым дополнительный колорит к смешению древней и современной Аравии.

يقضي بحارة سفن البوم الشراعية أشهراً عدة في البحر وهم يتنقلون على الطرق التجارية البحرية الرئيسية بين دبي وشبه القارة الهندية وإيران وأفريقيا. وتصطف تلك السفن لدى رسوها في خور دبي، في مجموعات متجاورة تضم كل منها أربع سفن. ويزور بحارة تلك السفن بعضهم بعضاً على متن سفنهم خلال الرسو، ويقيمون الولائم وحفلات السمر الليلية حيث يتجاذبون أطراف الحديث حول مجريات وأحداث رحلاتهم.

🇬🇧 Dhow crews spend many months at a time plying the ancient trade routes from Dubai to the Indian subcontinent, Iran and Africa, and back again. When they sail into the haven of the Creek, their captains, or *nakhuda*, moor alongside other dhows, perhaps four abreast, meeting up with old friends from other vessels. A visit during the early evenings will reveal much domestic activity on board each dhow, with meals being shared and coffee being drunk as the crews swap tales.

🇩🇪 Die Besatzungen der Dhaus verbringen lange Monate auf den alten Handelsrouten zwischen Dubai und dem indischen Subkontinent, Iran und Afrika. Bei ihrer Rückkehr in den Heimathafen des Creeks legen die Kapitäne, oder *Nakhuda*, Seite an Seite an andere Dhows an, um alte Freunde von anderen Booten wiederzusehen, sodass bis zu vier Dhows nebeneinander liegen. Am frühen Abend ist an Bord der Dhaus eine große häusliche Aktivität zu beobachten, während die Besatzungen zusammen essen, Kaffee trinken und Geschichten austauschen.

🇫🇷 Les équipages des boutres naviguent pendant de longs mois le long des anciennes routes maritimes commerciales entre Dubaï, le sous-continent indien, l'Iran et l'Afrique. Lorsqu'ils reviennent à l'abri de la crique, leurs capitaines, ou *nakhuda*, s'amarrent à couple à d'autres embarcations, sur quatre rangs parfois, et en profitent pour retrouver de vieux amis d'autres vaisseaux. Une visite en début de soirée révèlera l'importante activité domestique à bord de chaque boutre – les équipages y partagent leurs repas et y boivent du café tout en palabrant.

🇷🇺 Команды судов–*доу* проводят многие месяцы в плавании по древним торговым путям из Дубая к Индийскому субконтиненту, Ирану и Африке и только после этого возвращаются домой. Когда они входят в гавань Узкого Залива, их капитаны (*нахуда*) бросают якорь рядом с другими *доу*, по возможности борт к борту, порой неожиданно встречаясь со старыми друзьями с других кораблей. Дружеский визит ранним вечером друг к другу повлечет за собой значительное оживление внутренней жизни на борту каждого *доу*, когда члены команд совместно принимают пищу и пьют кофе, обмениваясь в то же время рассказами.

عربي لا تزال ضفاف خور دبي تجسد تقاليد دبي التجارية العريقة حتى اليوم بفارق وحيد وهو أن سفن البوم الشراعية باتت تعمل بالمحركات الآن. ويقبل الكثيرون من سكان وزائري دبي على ارتياد ضفاف الخور والحدائق المنتشرة حوله مع انخفاض درجات الحرارة قبيل الغروب، للترويح عن أنفسهم والتقاط الصور التذكارية.

The banks of the Creek evoke the city's centuries-old trading traditions with the colour and bustle of the loading and unloading of motorized dhows. It is a great place to enjoy a leisurely stroll during the cooler hours of the day as well as to capture some colourful photographs.

Die Farbenvielfalt und das geschäftige Treiben beim Be- und Entladen der Motordhaus am Ufer des Creeks rufen die jahrhundertealte Handelstradition der Stadt wach. Es ist ein phantastischer Ort, um während der kühleren Stunden des Tages gemütlich spazieren zu gehen und farbenfrohe Fotos zu machen.

Les rives de la crique évoquent les traditions commerciales centenaires par l'agitation haute en couleur du chargement et du déchargement des boutres à moteur. Il est agréable de s'y promener tranquillement pendant les heures les plus fraîches de la journée et d'y prendre de pittoresques photos.

Цветастость и сумятица, царящие на берегах Узкого Залива при погрузке и разгрузке моторизованных *доу*, навевают воспоминания о столетних торговых традициях города. Это замечательное место годится как для получения удовольствия во время неспешной прогулки в прохладное время дня, так и для получения красочных фотографий.

نشاهد في الجانب الأيسر من الصورة، مبنى المقر الرئيسي لبنك دبي الوطني بواجهته الزجاجية المحدودبة والتي ترمز إلى شراع سفينة. وقد صمم المبنى الذي يعد من أوائل الأبراج المكتبية المتميزة التي أقيمت في دبي، المهندس المعماري الفائز بالجوائز العالمية كارلوس أوتو. ويطل المبنى الذي تم افتتاحه عام ١٩٩٧، والبرج المثلثي الشكل الذي يجاوره (إلى اليمين)، والذي تتخذه غرفة تجارة وصناعة دبي مقراً لها، على سفن البوم الراسية في الخور ليجسدا تناغم الحداثة والعراقة في مشهد واحد.

The National Bank of Dubai building, on the left of the picture, with its curved façade of polished steel and glass, reminiscent of a billowing sail, was designed by award-winning architect Carlos Ott and was one of Dubai's first iconic buildings. Opened in 1997, the ultra-modern architecture of this building, as well as that of its neighbour, the triangular Dubai Chamber of Commerce and Industry building, stand in a complementary juxtaposition to the dhows below them.

Das Gebäude der Nationalbank Dubais, links im Bild, das mit seiner gebogenen Fassade aus poliertem Stahl und Glas an ein gewölbtes Segel erinnert, wurde von dem preisgekrönten Architekten Carlos Ott entworfen und ist eins der ersten Gebäude, die heute zu den Wahrzeichen der Stadt gehören. Die ultramoderne Architektur dieses 1997 eröffneten Baus stellt zusammen mit seinem Nachbarn, dem dreieckigen Gebäude der Industrie- und Handelskammer Dubais, einen interessanten Kontrast zu den Dhaus auf dem Wasser dar.

L'immeuble de la Banque Nationale de Dubaï, à gauche, avec sa façade bombée d'acier poli et de verre qui évoque une voile gonflée, a été conçu par l'architecte primé Carlos Ott, et fut l'un des premiers immeubles représentatifs de Dubaï. L'architecture ultramoderne de cet immeuble inauguré en 1997, ainsi que celle de son voisin, l'immeuble triangulaire de la Chambre de Commerce et d'Industrie de Dubaï, s'érigent en juxtaposition complémentaire avec les boutres à leurs pieds.

Здание Национального банка Дубая (слева на фотографии) с его выгнутым фасадом из полированной стали и стекла, напоминающим вздымающийся парус, было спроектировано архитектором-лауреатом Карлосом Оттом и стало одним из первых зданий-символов Дубая. Открытое в 1997 году, это сооружение с ультрасовременной архитектурой, как и соседнее с ним треугольное здание Торгово-промышленной палаты Дубая, построенное в таком же ультрасовременном стиле, показаны в дополнительном сопоставлении с располагающимися ниже *доу*.

توفر الجولة على متن أحد مراكب «العبرة» الصغيرة في خور دبي، أحد أفضل السبل للتعرف
إلى دبي في كامل روعتها وسحرها، حيث يشاهد المرء على ضفتي الخور تمازج القديم والحديث
في شكل مبهر. وتشاهد في الصورة إحدى محطات مراكب «العبرة» التي تنقل الركاب بين
شطري المدينة بر دبي وديرة المدينة عبر الخور، باعتبارها وسيلة مواصلات فعالة وشعبية وزهيدة
التكاليف، حيث كانت الوسيلة الوحيدة للانتقال بين الضفتين في الماضي غير البعيد.

The best way to enjoy the Creek is from the water and there's no better way to do this than take a trip on one of the many industrious water taxis, known as *abras*, which putter back and forth across the Creek – an inexpensive experience for the independent visitor. The *abras* provide a leisurely, old-fashioned way to travel in the very heart of a fast-paced, modern commercial centre. Pictured is one of several abra stations that are positioned along the Creek.

Die beste Art und Weise, den Creek zu genießen, ist vom Wasser aus, indem Sie eins der vielen geschäftigen Wassertaxis, oder *Abras*, die den Creek kreuzen, nehmen; eine preiswerte Erfahrung für den unabhängigen Besucher. Die *Abras* bieten Ihnen eine gemütliche, altmodische Form der Fortbewegung inmitten des schnellen, modernen Leben des Handelszentrums. Auf dem Foto ist eine der vielen Abra-Haltestellen entlang des Creeks abgebildet.

Le meilleure facon de voir la crique est de monter à bord de l'un des pittoresques bateaux-taxis, appelés abras, qui traversent la crique – une expérience bon marché pour le visiteur curieux. Les *abras* sont un moyen traditionnel et tranquille de voyager au cœur même du centre moderne et frénétique de la ville. Sur la photo, l'une des stations d'*abras* que l'on peut trouver le long de la crique.

Лучший способ получить удовольствие от Узкого Залива – это ознакомиться с его водной гладью, и нет ничего лучше, чем сделать это, совершив прогулку на одном из многих усердно работающих водных такси, известных под названием *абра*, которые снуют взад и вперед через Узкий Залив, – вполне недорогое удовольствие для самостоятельного туриста. *Абра* представляет собой неторопливый, старинный способ попутешествовать в самом сердце живущего в быстром темпе современного коммерческого центра. На фотографии показана одна из нескольких станций *абра*, которые расположены вдоль Узкого Залива.

قام الشيخ مكتوم بن حشر، حاكم دبي بين عامي ١٨٩٤ و١٩٠٦، بعرض إعفاءات ضريبية على السفن التجارية المبحرة بين دبي والهند، منتهزاً فرصة فرض إيران رسوماً مرتفعة على تلك السفن عام ١٩٠٢. وقد استقطبت هذه الخطوة العديد من تجار منطقة «بستك» الإيرانية للإقامة والعمل في دبي بصفة مؤقتة. غير أن نجل الشيخ مكتوم، الشيخ سعيد بن مكتوم، حاكم دبي بين عامي ١٩١٢ و١٩٥٨، قدم لأولئك التجار في العشرينات من القرن العشرين، منطقة قريبة من السوق الرئيسي للمدينة إلى الشرق من حصن الفهيدي، للاستقرار والعمل فيها. وقد عرفت تلك المنطقة الظاهرة في الصورة باسم حي البستكية.

In 1902, when high customs duties were introduced at Persian ports, Sheikh Maktoum bin Hasher, the Ruler of Dubai from 1894–1906, offered tax exemptions, which resulted in trade from India sailing for Dubai instead of the Persian coast. Many Persians from the area of Bastak migrated to Dubai on a temporary basis but, by the 1920s, Sheikh Maktoum's son and successor, Sheikh Saeed bin Maktoum, who ruled Dubai from 1912–1958, offered them an area along the Creek in which to settle. Located near Dubai's main souk to the east of Al Fahidi Fort, the new quarter, seen here, became known as Bastikiya.

En 1902, lorsque les ports iraniens introduisent des droits de douane élevés, Cheikh Maktoum bin Hasher, le souverain de Dubaï de 1894 à 1906, accorde des exemptions d'impôts ; le commerce commence à circuler par Dubaï plutôt que par la côte iranienne. De nombreux Iraniens de la région de Bastak émigrent alors de façon temporaire mais, à partir des années 20, le fils et successeur de Cheikh Maktoum, Cheikh Saeed bin Maktoum, qui gouverna Dubaï entre 1912 et 1958, leur concède une zone le long de la crique. Le nouveau quartier, montré ici, qui se trouve près du souk principal de la ville à l'est du fort Al Fahidi, est connu sous le nom de Bastikiya.

Als 1902 in den persischen Häfen höhere Zollgebühren eingeführt wurden, bot Scheich Maktoum bin Hasher, der in Dubai von 1894 bis 1906 herrschte, Steuerfreiheiten an, was dazu führte, dass der indische Handel sich von der Küste Persiens nach Dubai verlagerte. Viele Perser aus der Gegend um Bastak zogen zunächst vorübergehend nach Dubai, und in den zwanziger Jahren bot ihnen dann Scheich Maktoums Sohn und Nachfolger, Scheich Saeed bin Maktoum, der von 1912 bis 1958 regierte, ein Gebiet am Ufer des Creeks zur Besiedlung an. Dem neuen Stadtteil in der Nähe des Hauptbasars, oder Souk, im Osten des Forts Al Fahidi, wurde der Name Bastikiya gegeben.

В 1902 г., когда в персидских портах был введены высокие таможенные пошлины, Шейх Мактум бин Хашер, правитель Дубая в 1894–1906 годах, предложил налоговые льготы, которые касались торговли из Индии в направлении Дубая, минуя персидское побережье. Многие персы из области Бастака переехали в Дубай на временной основе, однако к 1920-м годам сын и наследник Шейха Мактума, Шейх Саеед бин Мактум, который правил в Дубае с 1912 по 1958 год, предложил им поселиться в районе вдоль Узкого Залива. Расположенный около главного базара Дубая, к востоку от форта Аль-Фахиди, этот новый квартал, видимый здесь, стал известен под названием Бастакия.

مشهد معبر لحي البستكية المطل على الخور وقد استعاد مظهره التراثي المتألق العريق بعد إعادة ترميم معظم مبانيه ومعالمه، حيث يوفر للزائر لمحة وافية عن نمط الحياة والمعمار الذي كان سائداً في دبي قبل اكتشاف النفط. ونشاهد في الصورة مسجد الحي الجميل وأزقته الضيقة والبراجيل الهوائية المرتفعة لمبانيه.

🇬🇧 The small Bastikiya district hugs the shoreline of the Creek. Now largely restored to its former glory, replete with a beautiful mosque, narrow *sikkas* (streets) and tall *barjeels* (windtowers), it offers visitors a glimpse into life of the more affluent people of Dubai before the discovery of oil.

🇩🇪 Der kleine Bastikiya-Bezirk zieht sich am Ufer des Creeks entlang. Nach einer umfangreichen Renovierung bietet der Stadtteil mit seiner schönen Moschee, den engen *Sikkas* (Straßen) und hohen *Barjeels* (Windtürmen) dem modernen Besucher einen interessanten Einblick in das Leben der wohlhabenderen Bewohner Dubais vor der Entdeckung des Erdöls.

🇫🇷 Le petit quartier de Bastikiya borde la crique. Il a été restauré et a aujourd'hui, en grande partie, retrouvé sa gloire d'antan, avec une magnifique mosquée, des *sikkas* (rues) étroites et des *barjeels* (tours à vent) élevées. Il offre aux visiteurs un aperçu de la vie des personnes les plus affluentes de Dubaï avant la découverte du pétrole.

🇷🇺 Район Малой Бастакии охватывает линию побережья Узкого Залива. Теперь, в значительной степени восстановленный в соответствии со своей прежней славой, с прекрасной мечетью, узкими *сиккас* (улицами) и высокими *барджеелс* (ветровыми башнями), он предоставляет гостям возможность кинуть взгляд на жизнь наиболее богатой народности Дубая в эпоху до открытия нефти.

تم بناء حصن الفهيدي الذي يتوسط الصورة ويعد أقدم مباني دبي، في عام ١٧٩٥. وبات الحصن اليوم متحفاً غنياً بالشواهد والمقتنيات التي تسلط الضوء على نمط الحياة في دبي قبل اكتشاف النفط. وقد تم استخدام الحصن في الماضي كمقر للحكومة ومستودع للأسلحة والذخائر وسجن.

Al Fahidi Fort, in the centre of the photograph, was constructed in 1795. It is Dubai's oldest building and currently serves as a museum with intriguing dioramas, life-size figures and sound-and-lighting effects, to depict everyday life in pre-oil days. In the past, Al Fahidi Fort has served as the seat of government, an armory and a jail.

Le fort Al Fahidi, au centre de la photo, a été construit en 1795. C'est le plus vieux bâtiment de Dubaï ; il héberge aujourd'hui un musée qui expose de fascinants dioramas, des figures grandeur nature et des effets de son et lumière qui dépeignent la vie quotidienne d'avant la découverte du pétrole. Dans le passé, le fort Al-Fahidi a été tour à tour siège du gouvernement, dépôt d'armes et de munitions, et prison.

Das Fort Al Fahidi, in der Bildmitte, entstand 1795. Es ist das älteste Gebäude Dubais und wird heute als Museum genutzt, das mit Dioramen, lebensgroßen Figuren und Ton- und Lichteffekten, auf verblüffende Weise den Alltag in der Zeit vor dem Erdöl darstellt. Einst diente das Fort als Regierungssitz, Zeughaus und Gefängnis.

Форт Аль Фахиди (в центре фотографии) был построен в 1795 году. Это самое старое сооружение в Дубае, служащее ныне в качестве музея с интригующими диорамами, фигурами в человеческий рост и звуко-световыми эффектами, иллюстрирующими повседневную жизнь в до-нефтяной период. В прошлом форт Аль-Фахиди служил местом пребывания правительства, арсеналом и тюрьмой.

تعد مدينة الأطفال الواقعة في حديقة الخور بدبي، خامسة أكبر المجمعات الترفيهية المخصصة للأطفال في العالم. وتشغل المدينة التي تتوسط حدائق غنّاء، مساحة شاسعة تبلغ ٧٧٠٠٠ قدم مربعة. وتوفر المدينة أروع فرص الترفيه واللعب التفاعلي للأطفال من مختلف الأعمار وتضم أربع مناطق رئيسية للعب إضافة إلى قبة فلكية ومسرح مكشوف.

🇬🇧 Children's City Creek Park is the fifth-largest 'infotainment' complex for children in the world. Covering an area of some 77,000 square metres and set among soothing greenery on the banks of the Creek, its primary coloured facility offers fun and interactive excitement for children of all ages through its four main areas of play, along with a planetarium and amphitheatre.

🇫🇷 La Cité des Enfants du Creek Park est le cinquième plus grand complexe d'« infodivertissement » pour enfants au monde. Couvrant une surface d'environ 77 000 mètres carrés parmi des ombrages verdoyants et apaisants, son installation principale offre amusement et expériences interactives aux enfants de tous âges avec ses quatre zones de jeu, son planétarium et son amphithéâtre.

🇩🇪 Der Children's City Creek Park, Dubai ist der fünftgrößte Informations- und Vergnügungspark für Kinder auf der Welt. Auf insgesamt 77.000 Quadratmetern umgeben von Grün wird Kindern aller Altersgruppen Spaß und interaktives Vergnügen geboten; neben den vier Hauptspielbereichen gibt es auch ein Planetarium und ein Amphitheater.

🇷🇺 Детский город в Парке Дубая на Узком Заливе является пятым в мире по величине комплексом "информационной поддержки" для детей. Занимая площадь примерно в 77000 кв. метров и расположившись среди успокаивающей зелени, он в самых ярких формах предлагает детям любого возраста веселые и интерактивные развлечения на своих четырех игровых площадках, а также в планетарии и амфитеатре.

عربي تتوفر حالياً ثلاث نقاط لعبور خور دبي بين ضفتي ديرة ودبي، وهي: نفق الشندغة وجسر المكتوم وجسر القرهود. ويعد جسر المكتوم أقدم جسور دبي، وقد تم افتتاحه في شهر مايو من عام ١٩٦٣، حيث وضع حداً لرحلة العشرين كيلومتراً التي كان يجب قطعها عند نقطة رأس الخور الواقعة في نهايته، للتواصل بين سكان الضفتين.

🇬🇧 There are currently three crossing points spanning the Creek from Dubai to Deira: Shindagha Tunnel, and Al Maktoum and Al Garhoud bridges. Al Maktoum Bridge, pictured, was the first bridge to cross the Creek and was opened in May 1963, ending the long, 20-kilometre trip by vehicle from Dubai to Deira (and vice versa) via the end of the Creek at Ra's al-Khor.

🇫🇷 Actuellement, trois points de passage permettent de traverser la crique entre Bur Dubaï et Deira : le tunnel Shindagha et les ponts Al Maktoum et Al Garhoud. Le pont Al Maktoum, sur la photo, a été le premier à enjamber la crique. Il fut inauguré en mai 1963, mettant fin au long voyage de 20 kilomètres qui passait par le fond de la crique à Ra's al-Khor pour aller d'une rive à l'autre.

🇩🇪 Derzeit gibt es drei Möglichkeiten, den Creek zwischen Dubai und Deira zu überqueren: den Shindagha-Tunnel und die Brücken Al Maktoum und Al Garhoud. Die abgebildete Al Maktoum-Brücke wurde im Mai 1963 als erste Alternative eröffnet und ersparte somit eine Fahrt von 20 Kilometern von Dubai nach Deira oder umgekehrt, um das Ende des Creeks in Ra's al-Khor zu umfahren.

🇷🇺 В настоящее время от Дубая до Дейры имеются три места переправы через Узкий Залив: тоннель Шиндага и мосты Аль-Мактум и Аль Гаруд. Первый из названных мостов, присутствующий на этой фотографии, был самым первым переправочным сооружением через Узкий Залив& он был открыт в мае 1963 года, завершив тем самым длинное, 20-километровое путешествие из Дубая в Дейру (и обратно) на машине через Узкий Залив у Ра's аль-Хора.

يخضع جسر القرهود الظاهر في الصورة إلى عملية توسعة كبرى ستزيد عدد حاراته من ست حالياً إلى ١٤ حارة عام ٢٠٠٨. وستستطيع كل حارة تمرير نحو ٢٢٠٠ سيارة في الساعة الواحدة. وسوف يتمتع خور دبي بنحو ست نقاط عبور خلال الأعوام القليلة المقبلة.

Al Garhoud Bridge, pictured, is being widened from six to 14 lanes. When complete in 2008, each lane is expected to be able to accommodate some 2,200 vehicles an hour. In the next few years, the Creek will have a total of six crossing points.

Le pont Al Garhoud, sur la photo, est en train d'être élargi pour passer de 6 à 14 voies. Lorsqu'il sera terminé en 2008, il pourra accueillir jusqu'à 2 200 véhicules par heure et par voie. Au cours des prochaines années, la crique bénéficiera de six points de passage.

Die hier gezeigte Al Garhoud-Brücke wird zur Zeit von sechs auf vierzehn Spuren erweitert. Nach der Fertigstellung im Jahr 2008 wird jede Fahrspur eine Kapazität von circa 2.200 Fahrzeugen pro Stunde haben. In den kommenden Jahren wird der Creek an insgesamt sechs Stellen überquerbar sein.

Мост Аль-Гаруд, показанный на этом фото, сейчас расширяется с 6 до 14 рядов движения. Когда эта работа будет завершена в 2008 году, то ожидается, что каждый ряд будет способен принять примерно 2200 машин в час. Через несколько лет берега Узкого Залива будут соединять уже шесть пунктов переправы.

عربي بعد فندق «بارك حياة» المجاور لنادي دبي للجولف واليخوت، أحد أبرز المنتجعات الساحلية الفخمة في دبي. ويشاهد في وسط يسار الصورة، مطعم «برودووك» المطعم الوحيد المقام فوق مياه الخور في دبي. ويبدو في خلفية الصورة النادي، الذي يستوعب مرساه ١١٥ يختاً وتحيط به العديد من الفلل، ومركز ديرة سيتي سنتر للتسوق، وهو أحد أشهر مراكز دبي الكبرى للتسوق. كما يظهر إلى أعلى الصورة مطار دبي الدولي، بينما تلوح في الأفق البعيد مجموعة من الأبراج السكنية التابعة لمدينة الشارقة المجاورة لدبي.

🇬🇧 The Park Hyatt hotel, nestled next to the distinctive Dubai Creek Golf and Yacht Club, is a luxury waterfront retreat. The yacht club is home to the popular Boardwalk, the city's only restaurant standing over the waters of the Creek, and seen in the centre left of the photograph. Above the yacht club's 115-berth marina and its villas is Deira City Centre, one of Dubai's most popular shopping malls while, in the distance, is the international airport and, further away, numerous high-rise buildings in the city of Sharjah.

🇫🇷 L'hôtel Park Hyatt, blotti auprès du caractéristique Dubai Creek Golf and Yacht Club, est une retraite luxueuse sur le bord de la crique. On y trouve le populaire Boardwalk, le seul restaurant de la ville qui surplombe les eaux de la crique ; au centre, à gauche. Au-dessus de la marina de 115 amarrages et de ses villas, on voit le Deira City Centre, l'un des centres commerciaux les plus populaires de Dubaï ; au loin, l'aéroport international ; et, au fond, de nombreuses tours de la ville de Sharjah.

🇩🇪 Das Park Hyatt Hotel, in unmittelbarer Nähe des erlesenen Dubai Creek Golf- und Yacht-Clubs, ist ein Luxusresort direkt am Wasser. Der Yacht-Club beheimatet das beliebte Boardwalk, links in der Bildmitte, das einzige Restaurant, das über dem Wasser des Creeks gebaut wurde. Über der Marina des Yacht-Clubs mit 115 Anlegestellen ist das Einkaufszentrum Deira City Centre zu sehen, eins der beliebtesten der Stadt; dahinter befindet sich der internationale Flughafen, und im Hintergrund erheben sich die Wolkenkratzer der Stadt Sharjah.

🇷🇺 Отель "Парк Хайятт", построенный рядом с очень примечательным "Дубай Крик Гольф энд Яхт Клаб", является роскошным местом уединения на берегу. Яхт-клуб вмещает в себя популярный "Боардвок"– единственный в городе ресторан, стоящий над водами Узкого Залива& он виден слева в центральной части фотографии. Выше прибрежной полосы яхт-клуба, оборудованной 115 причалами, и его вилл расположен Дейра Сити Сентр – один из наиболее популярных торговых пассажей в Дубае, а поодаль от него находится международный аэропорт, и еще дальше – многочисленные высотные здания в городе Шарджа.

عربي لقطة شاملة لمنطقة نايف في ديرة دبي، يظهر في وسط جانبها الأيمن سوق نايف الشعبي الذي
تم تحديثه بالكامل، بينما يظهر حصن نايف يمين السوق. وكان الحصن يستخدم في الماضي سجناً
ومقراً لأول مخفر شرطة في دبي، وهو لا يزال يلعب هذا الدور حتى اليوم.

🇬🇧 The Naif area of Deira, with its renovated, colourful souk to the right of centre. Naif Fort, seen to the right of the picture, was, at one time, a jail, and was home to Dubai's first police station, a role it maintains to this day.

🇫🇷 Le quartier Naif de Deira, avec son pittoresque souk rénové, au centre à droite. Le fort Naif, à droite sur la photo, fut jadis une prison et hébergea le premier poste de police de Dubaï, un rôle qu'il conserve encore aujourd'hui.

🇩🇪 Der Stadtteil Naif in Deira mit dem renovierten, farbenprächtigen Souk, rechts von der Bildmitte. Das Fort Naif, rechts im Bild, war früher ein Gefängnis und Dubais erstes Polizeirevier; letztere Funktion erfüllt das Fort noch heute.

🇷🇺 Район Найф в Дейре с его обновленным, красочным базаром справа от центра. Форт Найф, видимый в правой части фотографии, являлся одно время тюрьмой, и в нем был расположен первый в Дубае полицейский участок, существующий там до сих пор.

يعد دوّار برج الساعة أحد أبرز المعالم العمرانية في بدايات نهضة دبي الحديثة. وقد تم بناء البرج أوائل الستينات من القرن العشرين، فوق منطقة رملية شرقي ديرة وقرب ضفاف الخور. وتحيط بالبرج حالياً شوارع تكتظ بالسيارات ومبانٍ مرتفعة.

The Clocktower Roundabout is one of Dubai's original iconic structures. Constructed in the early 1960s on a deserted area of sand to the east of Deira near the banks of the Creek, it is now surrounded by tall buildings and welcomes motorists who have crossed Al Maktoum Bridge into Deira.

Le rond-point du Clocktower est l'une des structures représentatives originales de Dubaï. Il a été construit au début des années 60 dans une région désertique de sable à l'est de Deira, près des rives de la crique. Il est maintenant entouré de bâtiments élevés et accueille les automobilistes arrivant à Deira après avoir traversé le pont Maktoum.

Der originelle Uhrenturm inmitten eines Verkehrskreisels ist eins der Wahrzeichen von Dubai. Ursprünglich 1960 auf einem freien, sandigen Gebiet östlich von Deira, in der Nähe des Creekufers errichtet, ist er heute umgeben von hohen Gebäuden und begrüßt die Autofahrer, die Deira über die Al Maktoum-Brücke erreichen.

Часовая башня на Круговом пути – одно из первых сооружений-символов Дубая. Сооруженная в начале 1960-х годов на пустынной песчаной территории к востоку от Дейры, вблизи берегов Узкого Залива, она сейчас окружена высотными зданиями и как бы приветствует автомобилистов, которые переехали по мосту Аль-Мактум в Дейру.

يشكل مبنى بلدية دبي القريب من ضفاف الخور في ديرة، معلماً من المعالم العمرانية المتميزة العديدة التي تحفل بها المدينة. وقد أضيفت إلى المبنى في ثمانينات القرن العشرين، ساحة مظللة تقع وسط بركة كبيرة من المياه، لكي تضفي عليه لمسة من الجمال والطمأنينة.

The Dubai Municipality building, situated close to the Creek in Deira, is one of the city's many distinctive structures. During the 1980s, a shaded courtyard and water pools were added to the building to provide a peaceful ambience.

Le bâtiment de la Municipalité de Dubaï, situé à Deira, près de la crique, est l'une des nombreuses structures caractéristiques de la ville. Une cour ombragée et des bassins ont été ajoutés à l'immeuble dans les années 80 afin d'y aménager une ambiance paisible.

Das Rathaus von Dubai steht in Deira in der Nähe des Creeks und ist ein weiteres Wahrzeichen der Stadt. In den achtziger Jahren des 20. Jahrhunderts wurde es um einen schattigen Innenhof und Wasserbecken erweitert, um eine friedliche und gemütliche Atmosphäre zu schaffen.

Здание муниципалитета города Дубая, расположенное близко к Узкому Заливу в Дейре, является одним из многих примечательных городских сооружений. В 1980-х годах к этому зданию были пристроены затененный двор и водные бассейны, которые создают вполне умиротворяющую обстановку.

تحولت دبي في فترة قصيرة قياساً، من مجرد نقطة عبور لرجال الأعمال إلى وجهة سياحية متميزة تحفل بمئات الفنادق الفاخرة التي تمثل جميع شركات الفنادق الكبرى تقريباً. ويظهر في الصورة فندق هيلتون الخور، الذي يعد أبرز الفنادق الفاخرة المطلة على خور دبي.

Where once Dubai was a mere transit pit stop, the city has now become a tourist destination in its own right. Facilities available to visitors are second to none and almost all of the world's major hotel chains are represented, including Hilton, whose Hilton Creek hotel is just one of several grand edifices close to the Creek.

Mit der Zeit hat sich Dubai von einem einfachen Rastplatz auf den Handelsrouten zu einem regelrechten Tourismusziel entwickelt. Die verfügbaren Einrichtungen bieten höchste Qualität und praktisch alle großen Hotelketten der Welt sind heute hier vertreten, einschließlich des Hilton: Das Hilton Creek ist nur eins von vielen großartigen Gebäuden in der Nähe des Creeks.

Alors que la cité était auparavant une simple escale technique, elle est maintenant devenue une destination touristique à part entière. Les touristes y trouvent les meilleures installations, et presque toutes les principales chaînes d'hôtel du monde y sont représentées, comme le Hilton Creek qui est l'un des plus grands édifices bordant la crique.

Место, где город Дубай был когда-то простым транзитным пунктом, стало теперь по праву местом паломничества туристов. Гости обладают здесь непревзойденными возможностями, и почти все крупнейшие мировые гостиничные сети представлены в Дубае, включая Хилтон, чей отель на Узком Заливе представляет собой только одну из крупнейших построек рядом с этим водным путем.

عربي شجعت شهرة دبي العالمية المتنامية في عالم السياحة والاقتصاد، شركات سفن الركاب السياحية على إدراج دبي في قائمة وجهاتها السياحية المنتظمة. وتشاهد في الصورة محطة سفن الركاب المقامة فوق لسان من الأرض في منطقة الشندغة المتاخمة لميناء راشد. وتفصل منطقة بيت الشيخ سعيد التراثي بين المحطة وضفة ديرة من خور دبي.

🇬🇧 Dubai's growing reputation has encouraged cruise liners to include the city as part of their itinerary. Pictured is the ferry terminal adjacent to Port Rashid, which is located on a spit of land at Shindagha. Between the cruise liner and the Creek is the renovated Sheikh Saeed House area with its traditional windtowers and, across the Creek, is the area of Deira.

🇩🇪 Der immer besser werdende Ruf der Stadt hat dazu beigetragen, dass sie in viele Kreuzfahrtprogramme aufgenommen wurde. Im Bild ist der Fährenterminal neben dem Hafen Port Rashid zu sehen, der sich auf einer Landzunge in Shindagha befindet. Zwischen den Kreuzfahrtschiffen und dem Creek befindet sich das Sheikh Saeed House mit seinen traditionellen Windtürmen. Auf der gegenüberliegenden Seite liegt das Stadtviertel Deira.

🇫🇷 La réputation croissante de Dubaï a encouragé les bateaux de croisière à inclure la ville dans leurs itinéraires. Sur la photo, le terminus du traversier attenant à Port Rashid et qui se trouve sur une pointe de terre à Shindagha. Entre le bateau de croisière et la crique, on observe la zone rénovée de la maison de Cheikh Saeed et ses tours à vent traditionnelles; de l'autre côté de la crique se trouve le quartier de Deira.

🇷🇺 Растущая репутация Дубая поощряет круизные лайнеры включать этот город в свой маршрут. На фотографии показан паромный терминал, примыкающий к Порту Рашид, который находится на отмели у Шиндаги. Между круизным лайнером и Узким Заливом виден восстановленный дом Шейха Саееда с традиционными ветровыми башнями и с прилежащей к нему территорией, далее, за Узким Заливом располагается район Дейры.

عربي تستطيع الأرصفة المنتشرة في خور دبي استقبال السفن الصغيرة نسبياً، بينما ترسو السفن الأكبر مثل سفن الشحنات السائبة وناقلات النفط والحاويات في ميناء راشد الذي يتميز بعمق مياهه. ويقع الميناء الذي تم افتتاحه عام ١٩٧٢، بالقرب من مركز دبي، وهو يضم محطة لمناولة الحاويات وأخرى لسفن الركاب السياحية، ويوفر أكثر من ٣٥ رصيفاً لرسو السفن.

While the Creek can accommodate smaller trading dhows, larger vessels, including oil tankers and container ships, require sophisticated, dedicated facilities, such as those at the deep-water Port Rashid, which was opened in 1972. Located close to the centre of Dubai, the port has a container terminal, a cruise-ship terminal and more than 35 wharves.

Alors que la crique peut recevoir les petits boutres marchands, les plus grands vaisseaux, tels que les pétroliers et les porte-conteneurs ont besoin d'installations sophistiquées et spécifiques, telles que celles en eaux profondes de Port-Rashid qui furent inaugurées en 1972. Situé près du centre de Dubaï, ce port dispose d'un terminal de conteneurs, d'un terminal pour bateaux de croisière et de plus de 35 quais.

Der Creek ist für kleinere Handel-Dhaus schiffbar, aber größere Schiffe wie Öltanker und Containerschiffe benötigen spezielle ausgereifte technische Einrichtungen, wie sie seit 1972 von dem neuen Hochseehafen Port Said angeboten werden. In der Nähe des Stadtzentrums von Dubai gelegen, verfügt der Hafen über ein Containerterminal, zahlreiche Reperaturwerkstätten für Container, ein Kreuzfahrtterminal und mehr als 35 Kais.

В то время как Узкий Залив может принять только не очень большие торговые суда–доу, большие корабли, включая нефтяные танкеры и контейнеровозы, требуют сложное, специализированное оборудование – такое, каким располагает глубоководный Порт Рашид, введенный в эксплуатацию в 1972 году. Расположенный близко к центру Дубая, этот порт имеет контейнерный терминал, многочисленные мастерские по ремонту контейнеров, терминал для круизных кораблей и более 35 причалов.

اتسع نطاق خبرات وتسهيلات دبي الخاصة بالخدمات البحرية، لتضم صيانة وإصلاح السفن. ويبدو في الصورة حوض دبي الجاف الذي تم افتتاحه في سبعينات القرن العشرين ليكون واحداً من أكبر الأحواض الجافة في العالم. وقد استقبل الحوض سفناً من أكثر من ٤٠ دولة حتى اليوم، ويستطيع استقبال سفن عملاقة تصل حمولة الواحدة منها إلى مليون طن.

Dubai's maritime expertise has been expanded to include ship maintenance and repair. Dubai Dry Docks also opened in the 1970s and is one of the world's largest ship-repair yards. It has seen ships from more than 40 countries and has the ability to accommodate vessels of up to one-million tonnes.

Die maritime Sachkenntnis Dubais schließt heutzutage auch die Wartung und Reparatur der Schiffe ein. Die Dubai Trockendocks wurden ebenfalls in den 70er Jahren eröffnet und gehören zu den größten Schiffsreparaturanlagen der Welt. Schiffe aus über 40 Ländern wurden hier repariert. Es können Schiffe mit bis zu einer Million Tonnen aufgenommen werden.

Les compétences maritimes de Dubaï ont été étendues et comprennent l'entretien et la réparation de navires. Dubai Dry Docks a aussi été inauguré dans les années 70. C'est l'un des plus importants chantiers de réparation navale du monde. Il a déjà reçu la visite de bateaux de plus de 40 pays et peut recevoir des navires allant jusqu'à un million de tonneaux.

Морское обслуживание в Дубае было расширено до технического обслуживания и ремонта кораблей. Дубайские Сухие доки также открылись в 1970-х годах и являются одним из крупнейших в мире парков по ремонту кораблей. Они видели корабли из более чем 40 стран мира и обладают возможностью принимать суда водоизмещением до одного миллиона тонн.

عربي بدأت قيادة دبي الرشيدة الاستعداد لمواجهة عصر ما بعد النفط منذ سنوات عدة، وذلك من خلال تنويع القاعدة الاقتصادية للإمارة وعدم الاعتماد المفرط على دخل النفط الناضب. ومما يؤكد نجاح هذا التحرك، تجاوز دخل الإمارة غير النفطي لدخلها النفطي.

Dubai's leaders have spent many years preparing for the day when oil runs out, ensuring the emirate diversifies its economy from oil. Testimony to the success of this carefully planned diversification programme is the value of Dubai's non-oil exports, which now exceed those of the petroleum sector.

Die Staatsmänner Dubais bereiten sich schon seit vielen Jahren auf die Zeit vor, in der es kein Erdöl mehr geben wird, indem sie die Wirtschaft der Emirate diversifizieren. Der Erfolg dieser Strategie ist an den Zahlen der Nicht-Öl-Exporte abzulesen, die inzwischen die der Ölbranche übersteigen.

Les dirigeants de Dubaï se préparent depuis de nombreuses années pour le jour où le pétrole s'épuisera, en assurant la diversification de l'économie de l'Émirat. Le montant des exportations de Dubaï non-liées au pétrole excède désormais celui du secteur pétrolier, témoignant ainsi du succès de ce programme de diversification si soigneusement élaboré.

Руководители Дубая потратили много лет на подготовку того дня, когда нефть выйдет наружу, обеспечивая, таким образом, всестороннее развитие экономики эмирата, чтобы избежать серьезной зависимости от нефтедобычи. Свидетельством успеха этой тщательно спланированной программы разнообразного экономического развития является стоимость товаров не-нефтяного экспорта из Дубая, которая теперь превосходит стоимость экспортных продуктов местного нефтяного сектора экономики.

عربي تحولت دبي إلى مركز إقليمي رئيسي للطيران، بفضل استثماراتها الكبيرة في قطاعات الأعمال والطيران والسياحة. ويجسد التصميم المستقبلي المتطاول لقاعة الشيخ راشد للركاب والبرج الفريد الذي يعلوها، تطلعات دبي المستقبلية في شتى المجالات. وقد استخدم المطار نحو ٢٩ مليون راكب وارتفع عدد شركات الطيران التي تتعامل معه إلى ١١٣ شركة عام ٢٠٠٦. ومن المتوقع أن تؤدي عمليات التوسعة الراهنة إلى ارتفاع عدد الركاب الذين يستطيع المطار التعامل معهم إلى ٧٠ مليون راكب بحلول عام ٢٠٠٨.

🇬🇧 Dubai has been transformed into a regional aviation hub with heavy investment in business, aviation and tourism. Symbolic of the emirate's futuristic outlook is the elongated shape of Sheikh Rashid Terminal and its unique control tower. Nearly 29-million passengers passed through the airport in 2006, and by 2008, the current expansion plans will allow 70-million passengers. In 2006, 113 airlines and 25 charter airlines, flying to more than 160 destinations, used the airport.

🇫🇷 Dubaï est devenu un pôle régional avec de lourds investissements en affaires, aviation et tourisme. La forme allongée du Terminal Sheikh Rashid et son unique tour de contrôle, inaugurés en 2000, symbolisent les perspectives futuristes de Dubaï. Près de 29 millions de passagers ont transité en 2006, et d'ici 2008, les plans d'expansion permettront à 70 millions de passagers de transiter. En 2006, l'aéroport a accueilli 113 compagnies aériennes et 25 compagnies de charters, qui effectuaient des vols vers plus de 160 destinations.

🇩🇪 Dubai hat sich durch umfangreiche Investitionen in Unternehmen, Luftfahrt und Tourismus zu einem bedeutenden regionalen Angelpunkt des Luftverkehrs entwickelt. Die langgestreckte Form des Sheikh Rashid Terminals und der originelle Kontrollturm des Flughafens sind Symbole der futuristischen Zukunft des Emirats. Im Jahr 2006 verbuchte der Flughafen circa 29 Millionen Passagiere, und durch die derzeit geplante Erweiterung wird die Kapazität bis 2008 auf 70 Millionen erhöht werden. Zur Zeit verbinden 113 Fluggesellschaften und 25 Chartergesellschaften Dubai mit über 160 Zielen auf der ganzen Welt.

🇷🇺 Дубай превратился в региональный авиационный центр с серьезными вложениями в бизнес, авиацию и туризм. Удлиненная форма Терминала имени Шейха Рашида и его уникальная контрольная башня символизируют футуристические перспективы эмирата. Около 29 миллионов пассажиров прошли через аэропорт в 2006 году, а к 2008 году реализация текущих планов по его расширению позволит довести общее количество обслуженных пассажиров до 70 миллионов в год. В 2006 году 113 регулярных и 25 чартерных авиалиний в более чем 160 пунктов назначения воспользовались этим аэропортом.

يخضع مطار دبي الدولي إلى عملية توسعة شاملة، تشمل بناء محطتي الركاب الجديدتين ٢ و٣ ومبنى الركاب رقم ٣. وسوف يتمكن المطار لدى إنجاز هذه المباني الثلاثة عام ٢٠٠٧، من التعامل مع ٧٠ مليون راكب سنوياً. ويجري حالياً بناء مطار جديد في دبي. ويقع المطار الذي أطلق عليه اسم مطار عالم دبي المركزي الدولي، جنوبي دبي في منطقة جبل علي. وسوف يكون المطار لدى اكتمال بنائه وتشغيله عام ٢٠٠٨، أكبر مطارات العالم بمساحته البالغة ١٤٠ كيلومتراً مربعاً (ضعف مساحة جزيرة هونغ كونغ)، وسيكون قادراً على مناولة ١٢ مليون طن من البضائع والتعامل مع ١٢٠ مليون راكب سنوياً، وهو ما يتجاوز مجموع سكان المملكة المتحدة وأستراليا وكندا وسويسرا مجتمعين.

🇬🇧 An expansion programme is currently under way to construct the new Emirates-dedicated Concourse 2 and 3 and Terminal 3, which is set for completion in 2007 and will have the capacity to accommodate 70-million passengers a year. The construction of another airport is currently under way. Dubai World Central International Airport, located south of the city in Jebel Ali will, when complete in 2008, be the largest airport in the world, covering 140 square kilometres (twice the size of Hong Kong island). It will be able to handle more than 12-million tonnes of cargo and cater to 120-million passengers per year, more than the entire populations of the UK, Australia, Canada and Switzerland combined.

🇫🇷 Un programme de développement est actuellement en cours pour construire les nouvelles aérogares 2 et 3 et le Terminal 3, dédiés exclusivement à la compagnie Emirates, et dont la finalisation est prévue en 2007. Elles pourront accueillir jusqu'à 70 millions de passagers par an. Un autre aéroport est aussi en train d'être construit. L'aéroport international Dubai World Central, situé au sud de la ville à Jebel Ali sera, une fois terminé en 2008, le plus grand aéroport au monde, et couvrira 140 kilomètres carrés (deux fois la surface de l'île de Hong Kong). Il pourra manipuler plus de 12 millions de tonnes de fret et accueillir 120 millions de passagers par an, ce qui représente plus de l'ensemble des populations du Royaume-Uni, de l'Australie, du Canada et de la Suisse réunies.

🇩🇪 Das derzeitige Programm zum Flughafenausbau sieht eine zweite und dritte Rollbahn sowie ein drittes Terminal vor. Die Fertigstellung ist für 2007 vorgesehen und bedeutet eine Kapazität von 70 Millionen Passagieren pro Jahr. Darüber hinaus wird bereits ein weiterer Flughafen gebaut. Der Dubai World Central International Airport in Jebel Ali, im Süden von Dubai, soll 2008 fertiggestellt werden und wird mit 140 Quadratkilometern (zweimal so groß wie die Insel Hong Kong) der größte Flughafen der Welt sein. Er wird eine jährliche Kapazität von über 12 Millionen Tonnen Frachtgut und 120 Millionen Passagiere haben, mehr als die Bevölkerung von Großbritannien, Australien, Kanada und der Schweiz zusammen.

🇷🇺 В рамках программы по расширению аэропорта в настоящее время ведутся работы по строительству новых специализированных Главных залов 2 и 3, а также Терминала 3, которые должны быть завершены в 2007 году и которые получат способность принять 70 миллионов пассажиров в год. Сейчас идет строительство еще одного аэропорта. "Дубай Уорлд Сентрал Интернейшнл Эйрпорт", располагающийся к югу от города, в Джебель Али и занимающий площадь в 140 квадратных километров (т. е. в два раз больше острова Гонконг), станет после его вступления в строй в 2008 году самым большим аэропортом в мире. Он сможет справиться с более чем 12 миллионами тонн груза и обслужить до 120 миллионов пассажиров в год – это больше, чем население Объединенного Королевства, Австралии, Канады и Швейцарии, вместе взятых.

عربي يستضيف حي الكرامة الذي يتوسط هذه الصورة، سوق الكرامة الشهير والذي يضم مناطق مسقوفة وأخرى مكشوفة ويوفر شتى أنواع السلع بأسعار تخضع للمساومة. ويشاهد في أعلى خلفية الصورة خور دبي وضفة ديرة من دبي، بينما تلوح مدينة الشارقة في الأفق البعيد في الزاوية اليمنى من أعلى الصورة.

Dubai's Karama district and, pictured in the centre of the photograph, the ever-popular Karama Market, an indoor and outdoor shopping complex, where you can purchase almost anything and haggling is a must. Dubai Creek and Deira can once again be seen in the background, together with the city of Sharjah on the right-hand horizon.

Le quartier Karama, au centre de la photo, et le souk toujours très animé de Karama, un complexe commercial extérieur et intérieur où l'on peut presque tout acheter ; et n'oubliez surtout pas de marchander! Au fond, on aperçoit à nouveau la crique, Deira et la ville de Sharjah à droite, à l'horizon.

Der Stadtteil Karama und sein vielbesuchter Markt, in der Bildmitte, wo sowohl überdacht als auch unter freiem Himmel praktisch alles Mögliche gekauft werden kann. Feilschen ist hier unumgänglich. Im Hintergrund sind der Dubai Creek und Deira zu sehen, und am Horizont rechts befindet sich die Stadt Sharjah.

Дубайский район Карама и расположенный в центре фотографии неизменно популярный Карамский рынок – магазинный комплекс закрыто–открытого типа, где вы можете купить почти все и поторговаться. Это как раз то место, которое надо обязательно посетить. Узкий Залив и Дейру можно снова увидеть на заднем плане, вместе с городом Шарджа (на горизонте справа).

لقطة معبرة لشارع الشيخ زايد تؤكد حقيقة امتلاك دبي إحدى أفضل شبكات الطرق السريعة في المنطقة، التي تربط الإمارة مع الإمارات والدول المجاورة. وتبدو في الصورة ناطحات السحاب المطلة على الشارع، بما فيها برجا جميرا الإمارات إلى يمين الصورة اللذان يعتبر أحدهما بارتفاعه البالغ ٣٥٠ متراً، الأعلى من نوعه في الشرق الأوسط وأوروبا. كما يشاهد في مقدمة الصورة مبنى مركز دبي المالي الدولي قيد البناء.

Sheikh Zayed Road caught in the late afternoon sunshine. Dubai is a city of eclectism, with one of the best highway networks in the region, linking the city with its neighbours in the UAE and further afield. Soaring, elegant skyscrapers have risen from the desert sands to mingle side by side, including the distinctive Jumeirah Emirates Towers to the right of the picture. The taller of the two towers, at 350 metres, is currently the tallest building in the Middle East and Europe. At the foot of these towers, the Dubai International Financial Centre can be seen under construction.

La route Sheik Zayed, prise sous le soleil de fin d'après-midi. Dubaï est une ville éclectique, avec l'un des meilleurs réseaux autoroutiers de la région qui relie la ville à ses voisins des autres Émirats, et au-delà. D'imposants gratte-ciels élégants surgissent des sables du désert en se côtoyant ; parmi eux, les tours caractéristiques Emirates Towers, à droite sur la photo. La plus élevée des deux, haute de 350 mètres, est actuellement l'immeuble le plus élevé du Moyen Orient et d'Europe. En construction, aux pieds de ces tours, le Centre Financier International de Dubaï.

Die Sheikh Zayed Road im Sonnenschein des späten Nachmittags. Dubai ist die Stadt des Eklektizismus: Eins der besten Straßennetze der Region verbindet die Stadt mit ihren Nachbarn der Vereinigten Arabischen Emirate und in der Ferne, und hochaufragende, elegante Wolkenkratzer sind aus dem Wüstensand gewachsen, wie zum Beispiel die originellen Jumeirah Emirates Towers, rechts im Bild. Der höhere der beiden Türme ist zur Zeit mit 350 Metern das höchste Gebäude des Mittleren Ostens und Europas. Am Fuß der Türme ist das Dubai International Financial Centre zu sehen, das sich noch in Bau befindet.

Улица имени Шейха Зайеда, сфотографированная при позднем полуденном солнечном освещении. Дубай – эклективный город, имеющий одну из лучших в регионе дорожных сетей, которая связывает город с соседями в ОАЭ и далее с заграницей. Тянущиеся ввысь элегантные небоскребы поднялись от песков пустыни, чтобы стоять рядом, включая весьма примечательные Эмиратские башни в Джумейре (справа на фотографии). Более высокая из этих двух башен, 350 метров в высоту, в настоящее время является самым высоким зданием на Ближнем Востоке и в Европе. У подножия этих башен можно увидеть строительство Дубайского Международного финансового центра.

Another view of the most distinctive part of Sheikh Zayed Road and, to the left of it, Dubai's low-rise Satwa district. Sheikh Zayed Road continues out of the bottom right-hand corner of the photograph, and becomes the main highway to the island capital city of Abu Dhabi.

Une autre prise de vue de la partie la plus caractéristique de la route Sheikh Zayed et, à sa gauche, Satwa, un quartier de petits immeubles. La route Sheikh Zayed continue en direction du sud à droite de la photo et devient l'autoroute principale vers la capitale Abou Dhabi.

Ein weiterer Blick auf den charakteristischsten Abschnitt der Sheikh Zayed Road und weiter links auf den Stadtteil Satwa. Die Straße läuft an der rechten unteren Ecke aus dem Bild und wird zur Haupt-autobahn, die Dubai mit der Inselhauptstadt Abu Dhabi verbindet.

Еще один вид наиболее характерной части улицы имени Шейха Зайеда, а также, слева от нее, виден дубайский невысотный район Сатва. Улица имени Шейха Зайеда продолжается за нижний правый угол фотографии и становится там главной магистралью на пути в островной столичный город Абу Даби.

عربي راعت بلدية دبي لدى الترخيص ببناء ناطحاب السحاب في شارع الشيخ زايد، ضرورة توفير مواقف لآلاف السيارات التي يستخدمها سكانها. ونلاحظ في الصورة، وجود مبانٍ منخفضة قبالة كل برج سكني أو مكتبي، وهي مواقف متعددة الأدوار للسيارات.

🇬🇧 It's interesting to note that, while Sheikh Zayed Road's high-rise edifices accommodate the needs of people as places of business and as residences, almost all come with smaller, companion structures at their feet. These act as car parks.

🇩🇪 Es ist interessant zu beobachten, dass die hohen Gebäude der Sheikh Zayed Road, die der Bevölkerung sowohl als Büroraum als auch als Wohnung dienen, fast alle begleitet werden von niedrigeren Bauten. Dort befinden sich die Parkgaragen.

🇫🇷 Il est intéressant de remarquer que, si les grands immeubles de la route Sheikh Zayed répondent aux besoins des gens quant aux bureaux et aux logements, presque tous ont de petites structures à leurs pieds qui servent de stationnements pour voitures.

🇷🇺 Интересно отметить то обстоятельство, что почти все высотные сооружения на улице имени Шейха Зайеда, удовлетворяющие нужды людей в качестве мест для ведения бизнеса и для проживания, сопровождаются меньшими по размеру зданиями, которые используются в качестве автомобильных парков.

أدى نمو دبي الاقتصادي المتسارع والمستمر وما رافقه من انطلاق عشرات المشاريع العقارية السكنية والمكتبية فيها، إلى إحداث تغير جذري في ملامح المدينة التي قامت فيها عشرات جسور توزيع المرور والأنفاق والجسور والطرقات السريعة والتي لا يزال المزيد منها قيد التخطيط. وتشاهد في الصورة مستديرة مركز دبي التجاري العالمي، ويظهر إلى أقصى يمينها عمود تذكاري يعلوه مجسم للكرة الأرضية، أقيم تخليداً لذكرى استضافة دبي للاجتماع السنوي المشترك لمجلسي محافظي البنك وصندوق النقد الدوليين عام ٢٠٠٣.

As Dubai has grown, with numerous residential and business projects under way, so the urban landscape has changed to encompass flyovers, tunnels, highways and bridges, with many more projects planned for the future. Pictured is the busy, three-level Dubai World Trade Centre (DWTC) Roundabout, located at the foot of the building that shares its name. To the right of the photograph, a globed statue celebrates Dubai's hosting of the prestigious Annual Meetings of the Boards of Governors of the World Bank Group and International Monetary Fund in 2003.

Avec la croissance de Dubaï et les nombreux projets de constructions résidentielles et commerciales en cours, le paysage urbain a changé et comprend des voies surélevées, des tunnels, des autoroutes et des ponts. De nombreux autres projets sont en prévision. Sur la photo, le très fréquenté rond-point du Dubai World Trade Centre (DWTC), situé au pied de l'immeuble du même nom. À droite, un monument sphérique commémore la prestigieuse réunion annuelle des Conseils d'Administration du Groupe de la Banque Mondiale et du Fonds Monétaire International qui a été accueillie par Dubaï en 2003.

Mit dem urbanen Wachstum, das weitere Wohnungs- und Businessprojekte umfasst, die sich noch in der Ausführung befinden, hat sich die städtische Landschaft verändert: Überführungen, Tunnel, Autobahnen und Brücken; viele weitere Bauten sind noch in Planung. Das Bild zeigt den geschäftigen Kreisverkehr des Dubai World Trade Centre (DWTC), am Fuß des gleichnamigen Gebäudes. Am rechten Bildrand ist die Statue zu sehen, die daran erinnert, dass Dubai Gastgeber des Jahrestreffens der Weltbank und des Internationalen Währungsfonds 2003 war.

По мере того, как Дубай вырос за счет многочисленных жилищных и деловых проектов, изменился и городской ландшафт, не только включивший в себя путепроводы, тоннели, дорожные магистрали и мосты, но и продолжающий иметь дело с гораздо большим числом проектов, рассчитанных на будущее. На фотографии мы видим Круговой путь – оживленный участок дороги у подножия Дубайского Всемирного торгового центра (ДВТЦ). В правой части фотографии увенчанная шаром статуя напоминает о прошедших в Дубае в 2003 году престижных ежегодных встречах Советов управляющих Группы Всемирного банка и Международного валютного фонда.

عربي تم افتتاح مركز دبي التجاري العالمي الذي يشمخ برجه الأبيض المطل على بداية شارع الشيخ زايد إلى يمين الصورة، في عام ١٩٧٩، ليصبح أحد أبرز معالم دبي العمرانية وأهم مراكز أنشطتها الاقتصادية في الشرق الأوسط وسائر أنحاء العالم. ويظهر إلى يمين البرج موقع بناء فندق جديد يحل مكان الفندق القديم الذي كان قائماً فيه. كما يطل المركز من جهة اليمين على حديقة زعبيل التي أقيمت فوق أرض صحراوية، وباتت تستقطب أعداداً كبيرة من المتنزهين ومن هواة لعب الكريكيت خلال العطلات الأسبوعية في فصل الشتاء. ويشاهد إلى يسار الحديقة في الجانب المقابل من الشارع، البرج الجديد لمؤسسة اتصالات قيد الإنشاء.

🇬🇧 The DWTC, to the right of the photograph along the Sheikh Zayed Road corridor, was established in 1979 and has stood as an icon of the city and a focal point for business interests in the Middle East ever since. Behind the DWTC's white tower, the construction of the trade centre's new hotel to replace a previous incarnation is under way and, beyond the tower is Za'abeel Park, an area of desert that has been converted into parkland, now popular with visitors and winter weekend cricketers. Opposite the park, a new Etisalat telecommunications building is under construction.

🇫🇷 Le DWTC, à droite sur la photo le long du couloir de la route Sheikh Zayed, a été construit en 1979 ; il est devenu depuis, un symbole de la ville et un point stratégique pour les intérêts commerciaux du Moyen Orient. Derrière la tour blanche du DWTC, est en train d'être construit le nouvel hôtel du centre d'affaires qui remplacera son prédécesseur. Au-delà de la tour se trouve Za'abeel Park, une zone de désert transformée en parc, aujourd'hui très apprécié des visiteurs et des joueurs de cricket lors des week-ends d'hiver. En face du parc, un nouvel immeuble des télécommunications Etisalat est en construction.

🇩🇪 Das an der Sheikh Zayed Road gelegene DWTC, rechts im Bild, wurde 1979 eröffnet und hat sich seitdem zum Wahrzeichen der Stadt und zum Brennpunkt der Geschäftsinteressen im Mittleren Osten entwickelt. Hinter dem weißen Turm des DWTC ist der Neubau des zum Zentrum gehörenden Hotels zu sehen, der ein früheres Hotel ersetzt, und im Hintergrund befindet sich der Za'abeel Park, ein ehemaliges Wüstengelände, das heute viele Besucher anzieht und an Winterwochenenden als Kricketplatz genutzt wird. Gegenüber dem Park wird zur Zeit das neue Etisalat Telekommunikationsgebäude gebaut.

🇷🇺 ДВТЦ, показанный в правой части фотографии, вдоль улицы имени Шейха Зайеда, был открыт в 1979 году и с тех пор стоит в качестве символа города и центрального пункта деловых интересов на Ближнем Востоке. Позади его белой башни ведется строительство нового отеля Торгового центра, который должен заменить предыдущий, а за ней располагается За'абеель Парк – участок пустыни, превращенный в парковую зону, очень популярную среди гостей и игроков в крикет в период зимних уикендов. Напротив парка идет строительство нового здания телекоммуникаций "Этисалат".

يتوسط برجا جميرا الإمارات، القلب التجاري الجديد لدبي الظاهر في الصورة، ويتألفان من برج فندقي (إلى اليسار) يبلغ ارتفاعه ٣٠٥ أمتار ويضم ٤٠٠ غرفة، وبرج مكتبي يبلغ ارتفاعه ٣٥٠ متراً (إلى اليمين). ويتصل البرجان عبر طابق أرضي يشكل ردهة للتسوق ويضم العديد من المقاهي والمطاعم التي تستقطب العديد من الرواد.

The elegant Jumeirah Emirates Towers is located in the centre of the city's business district and consists of both a 305-metre, 400-bedroom hotel and 350-metre office tower. The two towers are connected to one another by a ground-floor shopping boulevard which, with its more than 15 bars and restaurants, is a popular destination for eating out.

Die eleganten Jumeirah Emirates Towers befinden sich im Zentrum des Geschäftsviertels der Stadt und bestehen aus einem 305 Meter hohen Hotel mit 400 Zimmern und einem 350 Meter hohen Büroturm. Sie sind verbunden durch ein Einkaufszentrum, dessen fünfzehn Bars und Restaurants ein beliebtes Ziel sind, um auswärts zu essen.

Les élégantes Emirates Towers sont situées au centre du quartier des affaires de la ville. L'une de ces tours, haute de 305 mètres, héberge un hôtel de 400 chambres. L'autre tour, haute de 350 mètres, abrite des bureaux. Les deux tours sont reliées par un boulevard commercial au rez-de-chaussée qui, avec plus de 15 bars et restaurants, est très fréquenté.

Элегантные Эмиратские башни Джумейры находятся в центре городского делового района и состоят из 305-метрового в высоту отеля на 400 мест и 350-метровой башни, занятой под офисы. Эти две башни соединены друг с другом по первому этажу бульваром с магазинами, который вместе с его 15 барами и ресторанами является популярным местом для тех, кто предпочитает не готовить еду дома.

اسطبلات زعبيل مقر اسطبلات جودولفين الشهيرة لتربية خيل السباق، كما تبدو تحت أشعة شمس العصر. وتعد هذه الاسطبلات الواقعة قرب أبراج جميرا الإمارات والتي تمتلكها أسرة آل مكتوم الحاكمة في دبي، من أقدم اسطبلات الخيل في الإمارة. وتحتوي هذه الاسطبلات على نخبة مختارة من الخيول الأصيلة والخيول العربية التي تقيم في ٩٠ اسطبلاً مكيفة الهواء، كما تضم مضماراً للسباق بمسافة ١٨٠٠ متر ومسبحاً للخيل يبلغ طوله ١٠٠ متر، يظهر أسفل الصورة.

🇬🇧 Zabeel Stables, the home of Godolphin, in the late afternoon sun. Located behind Jumeirah Emirates Towers, the stables are some of Dubai's oldest and are owned by the ruling family of Dubai. Home to both Thoroughbreds and Arabians, the horses live in five-star accommodation. Facilities include a 1,800-metre track, a 100-metre swimming pool, seen towards the bottom right of the photograph, and more than 90 fully air-conditioned stables.

🇫🇷 Sous le soleil de fin d'après-midi, les écuries Zabeel, la demeure de Godolphin. Situées derrière les Emirates Towers, ces écuries sont parmi les plus anciennes de Dubaï. Elles appartiennent à la famille régnante. C'est la demeure cinq étoiles des chevaux Purs-sangs et Arabes. Les installations comprennent une piste de 1 800 mètres de longueur, une piscine longue de 100 mètres, que l'on peut voir en bas à droite sur la photo, et plus de 90 écuries totalement climatisées.

🇩🇪 Die Zabeel Stables, Heimat des Godolphin, im Sonnenschein des späten Nachmittags. Die Stallanlagen hinter den Jumeirah Emirates Towers gehören zu den ältesten Gestüten Dubais und befinden sich im Besitz der Königsfamilie. Hier werden Englische und Arabische Vollblüter gezüchtet. Die Pferde leben in einem Fünf-Sterne-Luxus. Zu den Anlagen gehören eine 1.800 Meter lange Rennbahn, ein 100 Meter langer Swimmingpool, unten rechts im Bild, und mehr als 90 Ställe mit Klimaanlage.

🇷🇺 Конюшни Забееля, вотчина Годолфина, снятые при позднем послеполуденном солнце. Расположенные позади Эмиратских башен Джумейры, эти конюшни являются одними из самых старых в Дубае, а владеет ими правящий дом Дубая. Близкородственные как чистокровным, так и арабским скакунам, кони живут здесь в условиях пятизвездочного комфорта. Предоставленные им удобства включают трек длиной в 1800 метров, 100-метровый бассейн, видимый на фотографии справа внизу, и более 90 конюшен, полностью оборудованных воздушными кондиционерами.

تم استخدام ١٠ آلاف متر مكعب من الخرسانة في بناء عقدة الصفا المرورية الضخمة الظاهرة في الصورة، وقد تكلفت العقدة ٦٠ مليون درهم وتم افتتاحها للحركة المرورية عام ٢٠٠٢. وتحل العقدة التي تضم سبعة جسور مكان جسرين لم يستوعبا حركة المرور المتزايدة في دبي.

🇬🇧 Al Safa Interchange, which opened in 2002, utilized 10,000 cubic metres of concrete and cost nearly Dhs 60 million. The present incarnation of seven bridges replaced the original two, which were unable to cope with the ever-increasing number of vehicles on Dubai's roads.

🇩🇪 Zum Bau der 2002 eröffneten Al Safa Interchange wurden 10.000 Kubikmeter Beton und eine Investition von 60 Millionen Dirham benötigt. Die insgesamt sieben Brücken ersetzen zwei frühere, die nicht in der Lage waren, das ständig steigende Verkehrsaufkommen von Dubai zu bewältigen.

🇫🇷 L'échangeur Al Safa, inauguré en 2002, a demandé 10 000 mètres cubes de béton, et a coûté près de 60 millions de dirhams. Les sept ponts actuels ont remplacé les deux d'origine qui étaient incapables d'écouler le nombre croissant de véhicules.

🇷🇺 Для сооружения дорожной развязки Аль Сафа, которая вступила в строй в 2002 году, было использовано 10000 кубических метров бетона, а ее стоимость составила около 60 миллионов дирхемов. Нынешняя ее конструкция из семи мостов заменила первоначальную, состоявшую из двух, которые были не в состоянии справиться с постоянно увеличивающимся количеством машин на дубайских дорогах.

عربي يطل منتجع شاطىء وسبا دبي مارين على الخليج العربي من جهة وعلى طريق شاطىء جميرا من جهة أخرى. ويوفر المنتجع القريب من الوسط التجاري الجديد للمدينة، ١٩٥ غرفة وجناحاً و١٢ مطعماً لضيوفه، إضافة إلى شاطىء خاص وحدائق غنّاء. ويظهر في خلفية الصورة مسجد جميرا الشهير بتصميمه المعماري الإسلامي.

Nestled along the Arabian Gulf on one side and the Jumeirah Beach Road on the other, the five-star Dubai Marine Beach Resort & Spa is close to the heart of Dubai and offers 195 rooms and suites and 12 food outlets, along with its own secluded beach and verdant, landscaped gardens. Beyond it is the famous Jumeirah Mosque.

Niché le long du Golfe d'Arabie d'un côté et de la route Jumeirah Beach de l'autre, le Dubai Marine Hôtel est situé près du centre de la ville. Il offre 195 chambres et suites, 12 restaurants, ainsi qu'une plage privée et des jardins paysagers verdoyants. Au-delà, la célèbre mosquée de Jumeirah.

Der Dubai Marine Beach Resort & Spa liegt unweit des Zentrums von Dubai zwischen dem Arabischen Golf und der Jumeirah Beach Road und bietet den Gästen 195 Fünf-Sterne-Zimmer und -Suites sowie 12 Restaurants, einen Privatstrand und ausgewählte Grünanlagen. Im Hintergrund ist die berühmte Jumeirah Moschee zu sehen.

Удобно лежащий по побережью Аравийского залива, с одной стороны, и вдоль Береговой дороги Джумейры, с другой, пятизвездочный отель "Дубай Марин Бич Ресорт энд Спа" близко расположен к сердцу Дубая и предлагает гостям 195 комнат и многокомнатных номеров и 12 продовольственных магазинов, вместе с его собственным изолированным пляжем и укрытыми зеленью живописными садами. За ним находится знаменитая мечеть Джумейры.

يعد مسجد جميرا أحد أجمل المعالم العمرانية في دبي، ويشكل نموذجا رائعاً لفن العمارة الإسلامي المعاصر. ويستلهم المسجد تصميمه من مساجد العصر الفاطمي في مصر، وهو يضم مركز الشيخ محمد الثقافي. ويستهدف المركز الذي تم افتتاحه في مارس (آذار) عام ١٩٩٩، تعريف الزائرين بالمسجد وبمختلف جوانب الثقافة المحلية والحضارتين الإسلامية والعربية.

The Jumeirah Mosque is one of Dubai's most elegant landmarks and is a superb example of modern Islamic architecture. Constructed in the medieval Fatimid tradition, Jumeirah Mosque is home to the Sheikh Mohammed Centre for Cultural Understanding. Inaugurated in March 1999, the project aims to familiarize visitors to the mosque with various facets of local Arabic and Islamic culture.

La mosquée de Jumeirah est l'un des points d'intérêt les plus élégants de Dubaï. C'est un magnifique exemple de l'architecture islamique moderne. Elle a été construite selon la tradition médiévale Fatimid et héberge le Sheikh Mohammed Centre for Cultural Understanding (Centre Cheikh Mohammed pour la Compréhension Culturelle). Ce projet, inauguré en mars 1999, entend familiariser les visiteurs de la mosquée avec les différentes facettes de la culture arabe et islamique.

Die Jumeirah Moschee ist ein eindrucksvolles Beispiel für moderne islamische Architektur und eins der schönsten Wahrzeichen von Dubai. Sie wurde im mittelalterlichen Fatimiden-Stil gebaut und beherbergt das Scheich Mohammed Zentrum für Kulturelle Verständigung. Seit seiner Einweihung im März 1999 bemüht sich das Zentrum darum, die Besucher der Moschee mit verschiedenen Aspekten der lokalen arabischen und islamischen Kultur vertraut zu machen.

Мечеть Джумейры – это одна из наиболее изысканных достопримечательностей Дубая, являющая собой прекрасный образец современной исламской архитектуры. Построенная в средневековой фатимидской традиции, мечеть Джумейры тесно связана с Центром культурного согласия имени Шейха Мохаммеда. Начавшийся в марте 1999 года, этот проект преследует цель ознакомления гостей мечети с различными аспектами местной арабской и исламской культуры.

تفخر دبي بما تمتلكه من مراكز ومجمعات تسوق كبرى وعالمية المستوى. ويعد مركز ميركاتو للتسوق البادي في الصورة والواقع على طريق شاطىء جميرا، أول مركز تسوق من نوعه في الشرق الأوسط، تم تصميمه وفق الطراز المعماري الأوروبي في عصر النهضة.

🇬🇧 The emirate of Dubai boasts many impressive shopping centres and malls, including the vibrant Mercato Mall, located along the Jumeirah Beach Road. It is the first themed mall in the Middle East and is based on the Renaissance period.

🇩🇪 Das Emirat ist stolz auf seine vielen beeindruckenden Einkaufszentren wie beispielsweise das geschäftige Mercato Mall an der Jumeirah Beach Road. Es handelt sich hierbei um das erste themenbezogene Einkaufszentrum im Mittleren Osten, das sich an der Epoche der Renaissance orientiert.

🇫🇷 L'Émirat possède d'impressionnants centres commerciaux et galeries marchandes, parmi lesquels le Mercato, situé le long de la route Jumeirah Beach. C'est la première galerie marchande à thème du Moyen Orient : celui de la période de la Renaissance.

🇷🇺 Дубайский эмират гордится многими впечатляющими торговыми центрами и пассажами, в том числе единственным в своем роде Меркато Моллом, расположенным вдоль Береговой дороги Джумейры. Это первый "тематический" пассаж на Ближнем Востоке, архитектурные и некоторые другие особенности которого базируются на наследии эпохи Возрождения.

عربي يمتد طريق شاطىء جميرا بموازاة الساحل، الذي خضع مؤخراً لعملية تطوير وتوسعة منحته ثلاث حارات لمرور السيارات في كلا الاتجاهين، إضافة إلى العديد من الممرات المرتفعة المخصصة لعبور المشاة والمبنية من القرميد الأحمر وفق الطرز الأوروبية. ويشاهد في مقدمة الصورة منتجع وسبا جميرا بيتش كلوب.

The Jumeirah Beach Road, running parallel to the coastline, has recently undergone beautification and now has three lanes running in either direction, and numerous raised pedestrian crossings featuring modern, brick designs, as used in Europe. In the foreground is the Jumeirah Beach Club Resort & Spa.

Die Jumeirah Beach Road verläuft parallel zur Küste und wurde vor kurzem beschönigt. Sie verfügt nun über drei Fahrspuren pro Richtung sowie mehrere Fußgängerbrücken in modernem europäischen Ziegeldesign. Im Vordergrund ist der Jumeirah Beach Club Resort & Spa zu sehen.

La route Jumeirah Beach, parallèle à la côte, a récemment été embellie et dispose maintenant de trois voies dans chaque sens et de nombreux passages surélevés pour piétons avec des dessins modernes en brique, comme en Europe. Au premier plan, le Jumeirah Beach Club Resort & Spa.

Береговая дорога Джумейры, идущая параллельно линии побережья, недавно подверглась перестройке и теперь имеет три ряда движения в каждом направлении, а также установленные в большом числе пешеходные переходы, похожие на современные кирпичные узоры, используемые в Европе. На переднем плане находится "Джумейра Бич Клаб Ресорт энд Спа".

يوفر منتجع وسبا جميرا بيتش كلوب، بتصميمه البولينيزي ومبانيه المنخفضة الارتفاع وشواطئه الحالمة وحدائقه الاستوائية زاهية الخضرة، الملاذ المثالي للراغبين في الاسترخاء في مكان هادئ ولعشاق الرياضات المائية.

🇬🇧 The Jumeirah Beach Club Resort & Spa, with its Polynesian-style, low-rise buildings, tranquil beach and lush tropical gardens, is perfect for those wanting to relax, or for the more active visitor keen to try a wide range of water sports.

🇩🇪 Der Jumeirah Beach Club Resort & Spa besteht aus mehreren niedrigen Gebäuden im polynesischen Stil und verfügt über einen ruhigen Strand und üppige tropische Gärten; ein idealer Ort zum Entspannen und zum Praktizieren verschiedener Wassersportarten.

🇫🇷 Le Jumeirah Beach Club Resort & Spa, avec ses bâtiments peu élevés de style polynésien, sa plage paisible et ses jardins tropicaux luxuriants, sont un lieu idéal pour ceux qui désirent se reposer, ou pour le visiteur qui voudrait se consacrer aux différentes activités nautiques.

🇷🇺 "Джумейра Бич Клаб Ресорт энд Спа" со своими низкими зданиями в полинезийском стиле, тихим пляжем и пышными тропическими садами исключительно подходит для желающих расслабиться или же для более активных гостей, которые хотят попробовать свои силы в целом ряде водных видов спорта.

تشكل الفلل العصرية الفارهة المطلة على طريق شاطىء جميرا، الخلفية المثالية لمرافىء الصيد الصغيرة الواقعة على امتداد سواحل دبي، والتي تضم تشكيلة مدهشة من مراكب الصيد التقليدية ومراكب النزهة العصرية.

Modern, upmarket villas near Jumeirah Beach Road provide an interesting backdrop to one of the little fishing harbours along this stretch of Dubai coastline and its mix of traditional and pleasure craft in the foreground.

Moderne, luxuriöse Wohnhäuser entlang der Jumeirah Beach Road bilden einen interessanten Hintergrund für einen der Fischereihäfen entlang der Küste Dubais mit seiner Mischung aus herkömmlichen Fischer- und modernen Freizeitbooten.

Des villas de luxe modernes près de la route Jumeirah Beach servent d'intéressante toile de fond à l'un des ports de pêche le long de cette étendue de la côte de Dubaï, avec son mélange d'embarcations traditionnelles et de navires de plaisance au premier plan.

Современные высококачественные виллы около Береговой дороги Джумейры создают интересный фон для одной из рыболовецких гаваней вдоль этого участка побережья Дубая, а также причудливому смешенияю в ней традиционных и развлекательных судов на переднем плане.

مشهد ساحر لأحد شواطىء دبي الحالمة والقابعة في أحضان أشجار النخيل الوارفة، بينما تتجاور في الخلفية، المباني المنخفضة جنباً إلى جنب ناطحات السحاب العصرية. ويقبل سكان دبي وزائروها على حد سواء، على ارتياد شواطئها الجميلة للتمتع بالسباحة في مياه الخليج الدافئة، إضافة إلى شتى صنوف الترفيه والرياضات المائية .

One of Dubai's superb public beaches, with the low and high-rises of the city in the background. Residents and visitors alike are attracted to the warm, clear waters of the Gulf and all the usual modern water-sport activities are available.

Einer der hervorragenden öffentlichen Strände Dubais mit den niedrigen und hohen Gebäuden der Stadt im Hintergrund. Das saubere und angenehm warme Wasser des Golfs zieht Anwohner und Besucher gleichermaßen an und sämtliche üblichen Wassersportarten können hier praktiziert werden.

L'une des superbes plages publiques de Dubaï avec, au fond, les grandes tours et les petits immeubles de la ville. Les résidents et les visiteurs sont attirés par les eaux tièdes et transparentes du Golfe, où ils trouveront toutes les activités nautiques modernes.

Один из великолепных публичных пляжей Дубая, с низкими и высотными городскими домами на заднем плане. Жителей и гостей одинаково притягивают теплые чистые воды залива, доступны там и все обычные современные спортивные развлечения на воде.

عربي يشرف برنامج رصد سواحل دبي على إدارة تلك السواحل. وقد تم طرح البرنامج في العام ١٩٩٧ بعد تزويده بدراسة تضاريس قعر وأعماق مياه الخليج في منطقة جميرا. وقد أضيفت إلى البرنامج عام ٢٠٠٢ أجهزة لقياس اتجاه الأمواج وكاميرات فيديو معلقة فوق أعمدة مرتفعة على امتداد سواحل دبي بما فيها ضفاف الخور، بدءاً من بحيرة الممزر شمالاً ووصولاً إلى منطقة جبل علي جنوباً.

Dubai's coastline is managed by the Dubai Coastal Zone Monitoring Programme, which was launched in 1997 with a baseline bathymetric and topographic survey at Jumeirah. In 2002, the programme was expanded to include directional wave recorders and elevated video cameras along all of Dubai's coastline, including the Creek, from Al Mamzar Lagoon in the north down to Jebel Ali in the south.

1997 wurde ein Küstenzonen-Überwachungsprogramm ins Leben gerufen, das bathymetrische und topographische Messungen in Jumeirah durchführt. Das Küstenmanagementprogramm wurde 2002 erweitert, und Messgeräte für Wellenrichtung und erhöhte Videokameras wurden entlang der gesamten Küste Dubais installiert, einschließlich des Creeks, von der Al Mamzar Lagune im Norden bis nach Jebel Ali im Süden.

La côte de Dubaï est gérée par le programme Coastal Zone Monitoring, lancé en 1997 avec un levé de ligne de base bathymétrique et topographique à Jumeirah. En 2002, le programme a été étendu pour inclure des trace-vagues et des caméras vidéo surélevées le long du littoral et de la crique, depuis le lagon Al Mamzar au nord, jusqu'à Jebel Ali au sud.

Дубайским побережьем управляет Программа мониторинга прибрежной зоны Дубая, которая была начата в 1997 году с базисного глубинного и топографического обследования в Джумейре. В 2002 году эта программа была расширена за счет установления направленных волновых самопишущих приборов и усовершенствованных видеокамер вдоль всего побережья Дубая, включая Узкий Залив от лагуны Аль Мамзара на севере до Джебель Али на юге.

عربي تدين دبي بجانب كبير من ازدهارها وشخصيتها المتميزة إلى البحر والطرق الملاحية التجارية المحيطة بها والميناء الطبيعي لرسو السفن والتسهيلات التي وفرتها لتجارها. وبينما كانت مياه الخليج مصدراً للثروة السمكية واللؤلؤ على مدى العصور، باتت الآن توفر فرصاً أخرى في مجالات مختلفة مثل سباقات المراكب الشراعية التقليدية.

Dubai owes much of its prosperity, and indeed its character, to the sea and the trade routes it provided for the city's merchants. But the abundant natural resources of the warm waters of the Gulf also offer other opportunities. Traditional racing dhows, which compete in three different classes, are a familiar sight throughout local waters.

Dubaï doit une grande partie de sa prospérité et de son caractère à la mer et aux routes maritimes commerciales dont profitaient les marchands de la ville. Mais les abondantes ressources naturelles des eaux tièdes du Golfe leur ont aussi fourni d'autres opportunités. Des boutres traditionnels de course, qui courent dans trois différentes catégories, peuvent être observés habituellement tout le long de la côte.

Dubai verdankt einen Großteil seines Reichtums und seines Charakters dem Meer und den Handelsrouten, die von den Geschäftsleuten der Stadt genutzt wurden. Aber die reichlichen natürlichen Ressourcen des Wassers des Golfs bieten noch weitere Möglichkeiten. So sind beispielsweise auch die traditionellen Renn-*Dhaus*, die in drei Kategorien eingeteilt werden, auf den lokalen Gewässern häufig zu sehen.

Дубай своим процветанием и, разумеется, своим характером многим обязан морю и торговым путям, которые он проложил для городских купцов. Однако обильные природные ресурсы из теплых вод Аравийского залива предлагают также и другие возможности. Традиционные быстроходные суда–*доу*, которые соревнуются в трех различных классах, представляют собой привычное зрелище на всем протяжении местных вод.

تنتشر بمحاذاة حديقة الصفا (أعلى يمين الصورة) في منطقة جميرا، تشكيلة كبيرة من الفلل الراقية، وهو منظر كثيراً ما يتكرر في دبي، حيث تتداخل الحدائق مع المناطق السكنية. وقد تم افتتاح حديقة الصفا التي تبلغ مساحتها ٦٠ هكتاراً، أمام الجمهور عام ١٩٧٥، إحدى أقدم وأشهر حدائق دبي وأكثرها شعبية.

🇬🇧 Well-established villas in the area adjacent to Safa Park, which can be seen at the top right of the photograph. Throughout Dubai, the urban landscape is dotted with parks and gardens, and Safa Park, opened in 1975 and covering an area of more than 60 hectares, is Dubai's oldest and most popular.

🇫🇷 En haut à gauche, des villas bien établies dans la zone adjacente au Safa Park. Partout dans Dubaï, le paysage urbain est parsemé de parcs et de jardins ; le Safa Park, ouvert en 1975 et couvrant une surface de plus de 60 hectares, est le parc le plus ancien et le plus convoité de Dubaï.

🇩🇪 Die Gegend um den Safa Park, oben rechts im Bild, wird von wohlhabenden Einfamilienhäusern beherrscht. In ganz Dubai ist die städtische Landschaft von Parks und Gärten durchsetzt. Der 1975 eingeweihte Safa Park, der über 60 Hektar groß ist, ist Dubais ältester und beliebtester Park.

🇷🇺 Хорошо известные виллы на территории, прилежащей к парку Сафа, который можно видеть в верхнем правом углу фотографии. По всему Дубаю городской ландшафт буквально усеян парками и садами, а парк Сафа, открытый в 1975 году и занимающий площадь более 60 гектаров, является старейшим и самым популярным среди них.

مجموعة من الفلل الفاخرة في منطقة الوصل في دبي. ويلاحظ في الصورة الفلل المزودة بمسابح خاصة، والتي تم تزويد أسطحها بخزانات للمياه ووحدات لتكييف الهواء، وهي تجهيزات ضرورية نظراً لتدني معدل هطول الأمطار في المنطقة.

🇬🇧 Upmarket villas in the Al Wasl area of Dubai, with landscaped gardens and swimming pools. With such little rainfall, Dubai's homes typically have flat roofs dotted with air-conditioning units, water tanks and satellite television dishes.

🇩🇪 Luxuriöse Wohnhäuser im Stadtviertel Al Wasl mit beeindrucken-den Kunstgärten und Swimmingpools. Aufgrund der geringen Nieder-schlagsmengen in Dubai haben die Häuser normalerweise flache Dächer, auf denen Klimaanlagen und Wassertanks installiert werden.

🇫🇷 Des villas de luxe dans le quartier de Al Wasl, avec leurs jardins paysagers et leurs piscines. Étant donné la faible pluviosité, les maisons ont généralement des toits plats, parsemés d'unités de climatiseurs et de réservoirs d'eau.

🇷🇺 Богатые виллы на территории Аль Васла в Дубае, с живописными садами и плавательными бассейнами. При таком небольшом выпадении осадков дома в Дубае обычно имеют типичные плоские крыши, оборудованные воздушными кондиционерами и баками для воды.

يحتوي فندق جميرا بيتش المصمم في شكل موجة متكسرة، على ٥٩٨ غرفة تنتشر في ٢٥ طابقاً. ويشكل الطريق المنتهي بمطعم مارينا سي فود ماركت للمأكولات البحرية التابع للفندق، قوساً وكاسر أمواج يوفر ملاذاً آمناً لمرفأ صغير لليخوت ومراكب النزهة. ويظهر في الصورة خلف الفندق، منطقة أم سقيم السكنية التي تتألف من مبان منخفضة الارتفاع، بينما نشاهد يمين الفندق حديقة وايلد وادي للألعاب المائية، والتي تنتشر فيها أكثر من ٢٠ لعبة مائية مثيرة على مساحة ١٢ فداناً.

🇬🇧 The Jumeirah Beach Hotel, sculpted in the shape of a breaking wave, boasts 598 rooms on 25 floors. The causeway to the hotel's Marina Seafood Market restaurant arcs languidly into the Arabian Gulf, creating a safe haven for a number of private yachts. Beyond the hotel is the low-rise area of Umm Suqueim while, adjacent to the hotel, and seen to the right of the photograph, is Wild Wadi, Dubai's popular water park, where more than 20 adrenaline-pumping aquatic rides cover 12 acres.

🇫🇷 L'hôtel Jumeirah Beach, en forme de vague déferlante, a 598 chambres réparties sur 25 étages. La chaussée pour arriver au restaurant Marina Seafood Market forme une arche langoureuse dans le Golfe d'Arabie et crée un abri sûr pour quelques yachts privés. Au-delà de l'hôtel se trouve le quartier à habitations basses d'Umm Suqueim. À droite sur la photo, attenant à l'hôtel, on peut voir le Wild Wadi, le parc aquatique populaire de Dubaï avec ses 20 attractions de sensations pures sur 5 hectares.

🇩🇪 Das Jumeirah Beach Hotel hat die Form einer sich brechenden Welle und verfügt über 598 Gästezimmer auf 25 Etagen. Der Damm, der zum Marina Seafood Market des Hotels führt, schwingt sich in einem Bogen in den Arabischen Golf und dient als Hafen für private Yachten. Hinter dem Hotel befindet sich der Stadtteil Umm Suqueim mit niedrigen Wohnhäusern, während direkt am Hotel, rechts im Bild, Wild Wadi zu erkennen ist, der beliebte Wasserspaßpark mit mehr als zwanzig Attraktionen auf einem Gebiet von fast 50.000 Quadratmetern.

🇷🇺 Береговой отель Джумейры, построенный в форме разбивающейся у берега волны, гордится своими 598 комнатами на 25 этажах. Путь в ресторан морепродуктов ("Марина Сифуд Маркет") при отеле имеет вид слабой дуги, направленной в Аравийский залив, создавая тем самым безопасное убежище для большого числа частных яхт. За отелем расположен невысотный район Умм Сукейм, тогда как к самому отелю прилегает видимый в правой части фотографии популярный дубайский водный парк Вайлд Вади, где более 20 вырабатывающих адреналин аттракционов для катания занимают площадь в 12 акров.

يعد فندق برج العرب من أبرز معالم دبي الحديثة. ويقع الفندق الذي تم افتتاحه عام ١٩٩٩،
فوق جزيرة اصطناعية قبالة فندق جميرا بيتش ويظهر أسفل يمين الصورة جانب من مدينة جميرا.

🇬🇧 Burj Al Arab, opened in 1999, is the icon of modern Dubai. It sits on its very own man-made island adjacent to its sister hotel, the Jumeirah Beach Hotel. A part of Madinat Jumeirah fronts the beach at the bottom right of the photo.

🇫🇷 Le Burj Al Arab, qui a ouvert ses portes en 1999, est l'icône moderne de Dubaï. Il est situé sur sa propre île artificielle, à côté de «son hôtel soeur», l'Hôtel Jumeirah Beach. Une partie de Madinat Jumeirah fait face à la plage, en bas à droite sur la photo.

🇩🇪 Das 1999 eröffnete Burj Al Arab Hotel ist das Wahrzeichen des modernen Dubai. Es steht auf seiner eigenen künstlichen Insel, ganz in der Nähe des Jumeirah Beach Hotels. Ein Teil des Madinat Jumeirah ist am Strand unten rechts im Bild zu sehen.

🇷🇺 Бурж Аль Араб, открытый в 1999 году, является символом современного Дубая. Он стоит на искусственном острове, рядом с организационно связанным с ним Береговым отелем Джумейры. Выходящая к пляжу часть Мадинат Джумейры видна на нижней части фотографии.

تعد دبي واحدة من المدن التي تستضيف فنادق من فئة السبعة نجوم مثل فندق برج العرب الظاهر في لقطات مختلفة في الصفحة المقابلة، والذي يقتصر على الأجنحة فقط. ويبلغ ارتفاع البرج الذي يشكل الفندق والذي استضاف عدداً كبيراً من مشاهير العالم، ٣٢٠ متراً.

🇬🇧 Dubai is one of the few places in the world that can boast a seven-star hotel; the all-suite Burj Al Arab pictured here. A spectacular tower that soars to a height of more than 320 metres, its list of celebrity guests reads like a Hollywood roll call.

🇩🇪 Dubai ist einer der wenigen Orte auf der Welt, der über ein Sieben-Sterne-Hotel verfügt, das hier gezeigte Burj Al Arab. Sein spektakulärer Turm ist 320 Meter hoch, und das Gästebuch liest sich wie eine Aufzählung von Hollywood-Filmstars.

🇫🇷 Dubaï est l'un des rares endroits au monde qui peut se vanter d'avoir un hôtel sept étoiles, doté uniquement de suites, le Burj Al Arab. C'est un édifice spectaculaire qui s'élève à une hauteur de 320 mètres ; la liste de ses clients ressemble à une liste d'appel de Hollywood.

🇷🇺 Дубай – это одно из немногих мест в мире, которые могут похвастать семизвездочным отелем& здесь показан Бурж Аль Араб, оборудованный только многокомнатными номерами. Производит глубокое впечатление его башня, которая тянется ввысь более чем на 320 метров, а список его предыдущих гостей читается как своего рода сбор голливудских звезд на репетицию.

تنتشر على سواحل دبي تشكيلة كبيرة من الفنادق الفاخرة التي تستقبل ضيوفها في عالم فريد من الفخامة والرفاهية وخدمات راقية تهتم بأدق التفاصيل. ويتميز فندق «وان آند أونلي رويال ميراج» الظاهر في الصورة، والذي يذكرنا بقصور ألف ليلة وليلة بفخامة ديكوراته ومفروشاته وأجوائه الراقية وحدائقه الغناء التي تواجه جزيرة نخلة جميرا الاصطناعية.

🇬🇧 Luxurious hotels are scattered along Dubai's shores and guests, whether residents or visitors, enter a world where service, refinement and luxury are second nature; sophisticated places where no attention to detail has been overlooked. The One&Only Royal Mirage hotel is reminiscent of an Arabian palace and boasts luxurious interiors with a seductive ambience and beautifully landscaped grounds facing The Palm Jumeirah.

🇩🇪 An den Küsten Dubais befinden sich viele Luxushotels, und die Gäste, sowohl Anwohner als auch Besucher, treten ein in eine Welt, in der guter Service, Raffinesse und Luxus selbstverständlich sind. Hier wird kein Detail übersehen. Das One&Only Royal Mirage Hotel erinnert an einen arabischen Palast. Es bietet luxuriöse Innenausstattung, verführerische Atmosphäre und wunderschöne Gartenanlagen mit Blick auf The Palm Jumeirah.

🇫🇷 Des hôtels de luxe bordent le littoral. Leurs hôtes, résidents ou visiteurs, pénètrent dans un monde sophistiqué où le service, le raffinement et le luxe sont naturels, où aucun détail n'a été négligé. L'hôtel One&Only Royal Mirage, qui rappelle un palais arabe avec ses intérieurs luxueux et ses magnifiques jardins paysagers, fait face au Palm Jumeirah.

🇷🇺 Роскошные отели разбросаны вдоль берегов Дубая, и гости – местные ли они жители или же приезжие – входят в мир, где обслуживание, изысканность и роскошь занимают по важности второе место; это утонченные места, где уделяется внимание любой мелочи. Отель "Ван энд Онли Ройал Мираж", напоминающий собой арабский дворец, славится своим роскошным внутренним убранством с притягательной окружающей средой и прекрасно устроенными садами, выходящими на Палм Джумейру.

تتوفر تشكيلة كبيرة من العقارات الراقية في جزيرة نخلة جميرا التي تعد إحدى كبرى الجزر الاصطناعية في العالم، للتملك الحر. وتتألف الجزيرة الواقعة قرب فندق برج العرب، من جذع نخلة يبلغ طوله كيلومترين يتصل بالبر الرئيسي بوساطة جسر يشكل بوابة الدخول والخروج الرئيسية الخاصة بهذا المشروع العقاري الكبير. وسوف تستوعب سعف النخلة الست عشرة للجزيرة نحو ١٣٥٠ فيللا. بينما سوف يستضيف الهلال المحيط بالجزيرة والبالغ طوله ١١ كيلومتراً، نحو ٢٢ فندقاً ومنتجعاً.

Property on The Palm Jumeirah, one of the world's largest man-made islands, is available for purchase on a freehold basis and represents exclusive island living. Located adjacent to Burj Al Arab, The Palm Jumeirah consists of a two-kilometre-long trunk connected to the mainland by The Gateway Bridge. The 16 fronds, containing some 1,350 grand villas, will be home to more than 8,000 residents. Surrounding the fronds, an 11-kilometre arced Crescent will be home to some 22 luxurious hotels and resorts.

Der Grundbesitz auf The Palm Jumeirah, eine der größten künstlichen Inseln der Welt, ist käuflich zu erwerben und steht für exklusives Inselleben. The Palm Jumeirah, ganz in der Nähe des Hotels Burj Al Arab gelegen, besteht aus einem zwei Kilometer langen Stamm, der vom Festland über die Brücke The Gateway erreicht wird und von dem 16 Blätter ausgehen, auf denen circa 1.350 Wohnhäuser für über 8.000 Einwohner gebaut werden. Das Ganze ist umgeben von einem 11 Kilometer langen Dreiviertelkreis, auf dem 22 Hotels und Resorts stehen werden.

Les propriétés du Palm Jumeirah, l'une des îles artificielles les plus grandes au monde, peuvent être acquises en pleine propriété ; elles représentent le summum du luxe des îles. Attenant au Burj Al Arab, le Palm Jumeirah est constitué d'un tronc relié à la terre par The Gateway Bridge. Les 16 palmes, avec environ 1 350 villas, hébergeront plus de 8 000 personnes. Autour des palmes, un croissant de 11 kilomètres de long, en forme d'arc, abritera quelque 22 hôtels et centres touristiques.

Собственность на Палм Джумейре – одном из крупнейших в мире искусственных островов – доступна для покупки на основе безусловного права собственности на недвижимость и предоставляет исключительные возможности проживания на острове. Будучи расположена рядом с Бурж Аль Араб, Палм Джумейра имеет форму ствола длиной два километра и соединяется с материком по мосту Гэйтвэй Бридж. На 16 ответвлениях располагаются приблизительно 1350 вилл, которые станут жилищами для более чем 8000 человек. На окружающем эти ответвления 11-километровом дугообразном Полумесяце появятся примерно 22 отеля и курорта.

عربي تتسارع مشاريع البناء على قدم وساق في مختلف أنحاء دبي. وقد استدعت هذه الطفرة العمرانية غير المسبوقة تطويراً مستمراً ومتزامناً للبنى التحتية للمدينة. وتجسد هذه الطفرة النمو السكاني للمدينة، ورؤية القيادة الرشيدة بتحويل المدينة إلى تحفة عمرانية فائقة التفرد والإبداع على مستوى العالم أجمع.

🇬🇧 The pace of construction round the Emirate of Dubai continues unabated. The expansion of the city's infrastructure is vital to meet the increasing needs of a burgeoning population and to satisfy Dubai's vision and desire to create an innovative, monumental city that the world cannot fail to notice.

🇫🇷 Le rythme de la construction partout dans l'Émirat de Dubaï ne faiblit pas. Il est essentiel de développer l'infrastructure de la ville pour faire face à une population croissante et pour répondre à la vision et au désir de Dubaï de créer une ville innovatrice et monumentale que le reste du monde ne pourra manquer de remarquer.

🇩🇪 Die Bauaktivität im Emirat Dubai schreitet weiter ungebremst voran. Der Ausbau der Infrastruktur der Stadt ist für die zunehmenden Bedürfnisse der sprießenden Bevölkerung und für die Befriedigung des Wunsches Dubais, eine innovative, monumentale Metropole zu schaffen, die von der Welt nicht übersehen werden kann, von großer Bedeutung.

🇷🇺 Темпы строительства по всему Дубайскому эмирату не ослабевают. Расширение городской инфраструктуры жизненно необходимо для того, чтобы отвечать растущим потребностям увеличивающегося населения и удовлетворить мечту и желание жителей Дубая создать технически прогрессивный, монументальный город, которому сможет воздать должное весь остальной мир.

مدينة جميرا الظاهرة في الصورة، واحدة من أحدث مشاريع دبي العقارية المتميزة. وتتخلل المدينة المطلة على مياه الخليج، قنوات مائية يبلغ طولها أربعة كيلومترات. وتجسد المدينة التراث البحري العريق لدبي وماضيها الذي قام على التجارة، وهي تستخدم أحدث التقنيات العصرية لتجسيد فخامة الهندسة المعمارية العربية.

One of Dubai's newer developments is Madinat Jumeirah, set amid nearly four kilometres of waterways along a kilometre of beachfront adjacent to Burj Al Arab. It is a remarkable tribute to the emirate's sea-faring past and its historical roots as the City of Merchants. By using the latest technology, it effectively recreates the opulent side of old Arabia.

Eins der jüngsten Projekte Dubais ist das Resort Madinat Jumeirah mit einem fast vier Kilometer langen Netz von Wasserwegen und einem Kilometer Strand, ganz in der Nähe des Burj Al Arab. Es handelt sich hierbei um ein bemerkenswertes Tribut an die Seefahrer-vergangenheit des Emirats und an die historischen Wurzeln der Stadt der Händler. Mit den Mitteln der neusten Technologie lebt hier die opulente Seite des Alten Arabiens neu auf.

L'une des réalisations récentes de Dubaï est le Madinat Jumeirah, établi au milieu de 4 kilomètres de voies navigables le long d'une plage d'un kilomètre, attenant au Burj Al Arab. C'est un remarquable hommage au passé maritime de l'émirat et à ses racines historiques en tant que ville de marchands. Grâce à la technologie de pointe, il recrée l'opulence de l'ancienne Arabie.

Одним из недавних результатов развития Дубая является Мадинат Джумейра, созданная среди приблизительно четырех километров водных путей вдоль одного километра пляжного пространства, смежного с Бурж Аль Араб. Это замечательная дань уважения мореходному прошлому эмирата и его истории как города купцов. Благодаря использованию новейших технологий, Мадинат Джумейра эффектно воссоздает зажиточный стиль жизни в прежней Аравии.

واحدة من ٣٠٠ جزيرة اصطناعية تشكل أرخبيل «جزر العالم» ويحميها كاسر أمواج إهليلجي الشكل. وتتيح المشاريع العقارية التي ستقام فوق الجزر الواقعة على مسافة بضعة كيلومترات من سواحل دبي، فرصة تملك العقارات التي توفر أجواء مثالية للمراكب، لحياة الجزر السياحية الحالمة. ويلاحظ في الصورة، أن الجزيرة مزودة بمرسى خاص للنزهة ومهبط خاص بطائرات الهيليكوبتر.

One of the islands of The World, a 300-island, man-made archipelago, protected by an oval breakwater, located a few kilometres offshore. The islands are available for purchase on a freehold basis and represent the ultimate in exclusive island living. The island boasts its own jetty and helipad.

Eine der Inseln des künstlichen Archipels The World, einige Kilometer vor der Küste Dubais, das insgesamt aus 300 Inseln besteht und dem ein schützender ovaler Wellenbrecher vorgelagert ist. Die Inseln sind käuflich zu erwerben und sind in Sachen exklusives Inselleben nicht zu übertreffen. Diese Insel verfügt über eine eigene Mole und einen eigenen Hubschrauber-Landeplatz.

L'une des îles de The World, un archipel artificiel de 300 îles, protégé par un brise-lames ovale, situé à quelques kilomètres au large. Les îles peuvent être acquises en pleine propriété et représentent le dernier cri en terme de vie luxueuse. L'île possède son propre embarcadère et héliport.

Один из островов искусственного архипелага "Мир" ("Уорлд"), состоящего из 300 островов, который защищен овальным волнорезом и расположен в нескольких километрах от берега. Эти острова доступны для покупки на основе безусловного права собственности на недвижимость и предоставляют максимально исключительные возможности островного проживания. Данный остров знаменит своей пристанью и вертолетной площадкой.

تتغير ملامح دبي العمرانية بسرعة قياسية مع اكتمال العشرات من المشاريع العقارية الكبرى التي تقام فيها. وقد سمح للوافدين بتملك العقارات في بعض مناطق دبي منذ عام ٢٠٠٢. وتتوفر تلك المشاريع أعداداً كبيرة من الشقق والفلل المتميزة بأسعار منافسة على المستوى العالمي. وقد ازدهرت هذه السوق العقارية المتميزة بفضل الاستقرار الاقتصادي والسياسي وغياب الضرائب في دبي ودولة الإمارات العربية المتحدة، وما يوفره ذلك من عائدات مرتفعة للاستثمارات.

Dubai is a changing city and ambitious residential projects are continually being constructed. Expatriates have been able to purchase property in certain areas in Dubai since 2002 and apartments and villas of all sizes are relatively inexpensive compared to international standards. A stable economy, combined with a tax-free environment and the chance to take advantage of high returns on investment have provided the very best opportunities for this market to flourish.

Dubai ist eine sich schnell verändernde Stadt, die sich durch ständige ehrgeizige Wohnungsbauprojekte auszeichnet. Viele im Ausland lebende Bürger haben seit 2002 in bestimmten Gegenden von Dubai Wohnungen und Eigenheime in allen verschiedenen Größen gekauft, die im internationalen Vergleich relativ preisgünstig sind. Die stabile Wirtschaft des Emirats, in Verbindung mit Steuerfreiheit und hohen Gewinnen für Investitionen, hat beste Voraussetzungen geschaffen, um diesen Markt aufblühen zu lassen.

Dubaï est une ville changeante ; d'ambitieux projets résidentiels sont constamment en cours de contruction. Les expatriés peuvent acquérir des propriétés dans certains quartiers de Dubaï depuis 2002, et des appartements et des villas de toutes tailles sont relativement bon marché par rapport aux prix internationaux. Une économie stable, un environnement sans impôt et la possibilité de profiter d'un taux de rendement du capital investi élevé ont permis à ce marché de prospérer.

Дубай – это изменяющийся город, в котором непрерывно реализуются амбициозные жилищные проекты. С 2002 года эмигранты могут приобретать собственность в определенных районах Дубая, а квартиры и виллы любых размеров здесь относительно недороги по сравнению с международными стандартами. Стабильная экономика в сочетании со свободой от налогов зоной и шансом получения преимуществ в виде значительных компенсаций при вложении капиталов создали самые лучшие возможности для процветания здешнего рынка.

عربي يقع مشروع مرسى دبي العقاري المتميز في قلب ما بات يعرف باسم «دبي الجديدة».
ويضم المشروع المطل على مرسى وقنوات مائية اصطناعية، المئات من الأبراج والفلل السكنية
الراقية. ونشاهد في الصورة، العشرات من اليخوت ومراكب النزهة راسية قرب إحدى
مجموعات الفلل التي يضمها المشروع.

🇬🇧 Dubai Marina lies at the heart of what has become known as 'New Dubai'. When completed, the development will boast a multitude of high-rise buildings bordering the man-made marina. In this photograph, a selection of luxurious private yachts are moored at the foot of several of the marina's villas.

🇫🇷 Dubai Marina se trouve au cœur de ce qui s'appelle le « nouveau Dubaï ». Lorsqu'il sera terminé, ce projet comprendra de nombreux immeubles le long de la marina artificielle. Sur cette photo, des yachts de luxe privés sont amarrés au pied des villas de la marina.

🇩🇪 Die Dubai Marina liegt im Zentrum des Gebiets, das „New Dubai" genannt wird. Nach der Fertigstellung wird das Projekt aus einer Anzahl von Hochhäusern bestehen, die an einer künstlichen Marina stehen. Das Bild zeigt eine Auswahl von privaten Luxusyachten, die vor den Wohnhäusern der Marina festgemacht haben.

🇷🇺 Дубай Марина лежит в самом сердце того, что известно теперь как "Новый Дубай". После завершения данного строительного проекта в этом месте появится множеством высотных зданий, окаймляющих искусственную набережную. На этой фотографии роскошные частные яхты стоят на причале перед несколькими виллами на набережной.

عربي لقطة معبرة تجسِّد التطور المذهل الذي شهدته مدينة دبي للإعلام منذ بداياتها الأولى، حين كانت تقتصر على ثلاثة مبانٍ تنتشر على شكل قوس، وتقع بالقرب من مشروع مرسى دبي ومشروع جميرا بيتش ريزيدانس العقاريين المتميزين والباديين من بعيد باتجاه الشمال انطلاقاً من أسفل الصورة. كما يمكننا مشاهدة مشروع نخلة جميرا العقاري الضخم وفندق «وان آند أونلي رويال ميراج» إلى يمين الصورة.

Dubai Media City, which has grown from the three buildings in an arc located adjacent to Dubai Marina, and Jumeirah Beach Residence in the distance. The Palm Jumeirah can also be seen to the right of the image, along with the One&Only Royal Mirage.

Dubai Media City, qui s'est développée à partir des trois immeubles en arc de cercle à côté de Dubai Marina, et Jumeirah Beach Residence au loin. À droite sur la photo, le Palm Jumeirah et le One&Only Royal Mirage.

Die Dubai Media City, die über die ursprünglichen drei Gebäude, bogenförmig neben der Dubai Marina angeordnet, hinausgewachsen ist, und in der Ferne die Jumeirah Beach Residence; rechts im Bild The Palm Jumeirah und das One&Only Royal Mirage Hotel.

Дубай Медиа Сити, который вырос из трех зданий в дуге, расположенной рядом с Дубай Марина, и, поодаль, Джумейра Бич Резиденс. Палм Джумейра также может быть видна в правой части изображения, вместе с "Ван энд Онли Ройал Мираж".

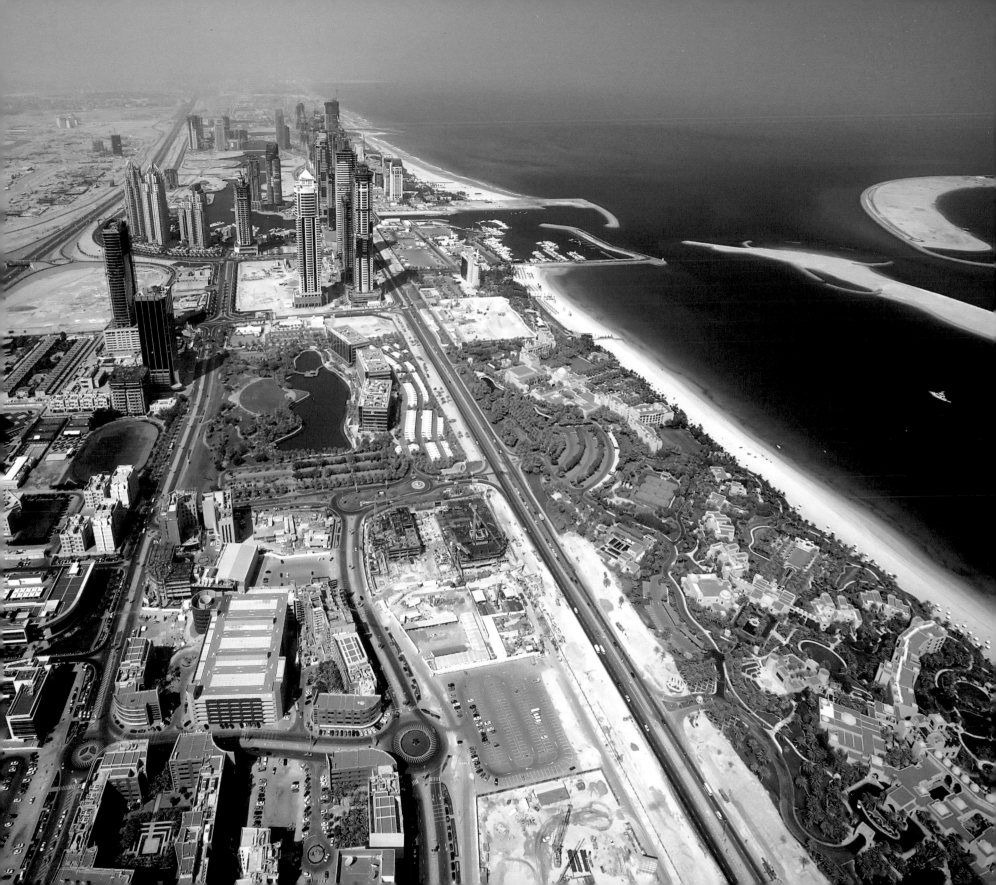

عربي يطل فندق لو رويال مريديان الفاخر فئة الخمسة نجوم والذي يتميز بتزويد جميع غرفه بشر
فات، على شاطىء جميرا. ويضم الفندق نادي سبا صحياً فاخراً مصمماً على الطريقة الرومانية.

Le Royal Meridien hotel reclines along the Jumeirah coastline and is one of Dubai's five-star resorts. Its facilities include a Roman-themed spa and its bedrooms all have balconies.

Das Hotel Le Royal Meridien steht an der Küste von Jumeirah und ist eins der Fünf-Sterne-Resorts von Dubai. Zu seinen Einrichtungen gehört ein Spa im römischen Stil und sämtliche Gästezimmer verfügen über einen Balkon.

L'hôtel Royal Méridien, le long du littoral de Jumeirah, est l'un des hotels-club cinq étoiles de Dubaï. Ses installations comprennent un spa à thème romain, et toutes les chambres ont des balcons.

Отель "Ройаль Меридьен" стоит вдоль побережья Джумейры и является одним из пяти-звездочных курортов Дубая. Его средства обслуживания включают горячую ванну в римском стиле, а все его спальные комнаты имеют балконы.

تستضيف دبي بطولة دبي ديزيرت كلاسيك للجولف التي باتت إحدى المحطات الرئيسية المتميزة في بطولة الجولف الأوروبية. وتقام البطولة على أرض ملاعب نادي الإمارات للجولف الذي تم افتتاحه عام ١٩٨٨. ويضم النادي ملعب المجلس الذي يعد أول ملاعب الجولف العشبية المخصصة لاستضافة البطولات في منطقة الخليج، والذي تمت توسعته ليتصل بملعب الوادي عام ١٩٩٥. ويظهر ملعب المجلس ومبنى النادي في الصورة، في شكل مجموعة من الخيام البدوية. وقد التقطت الصورة خلال بطولة دبي ديزيرت كلاسيك للجولف ٢٠٠٦، والتي فاز بها النجم العالمي تايجر وودز. أما ملعب الوادي الظاهر أسفل الصورة، وهو يخضع لعملية تطوير بعد أن أعاد المصمم العالمي نِك فالدو تصميمه بالكامل عام ٢٠٠٦ أيضاً،.

Dubai hosts the Dubai Desert Classic, now a staple on the European Tour, at the Emirates Golf Club. The club opened in 1988 with the Majlis course, the region's first all-grass championship golf course, and was extended with the Wadi course in 1995. This photograph of the Majlis course and the club house, shaped like a cluster of Bedouin tents, was taken during the 2006 Dubai Desert Classic, which was eventually won by Tiger Woods. The Wadi course, towards the bottom of the picture, was redesigned by Nick Faldo, also in 2006, and can be seen undergoing redevelopment.

In Dubai, im Emirates Golf Club, findet das Dubai Desert Classic statt, das inzwischen zum festen Programm der European Tour gehört. Der Club wurde 1988 gegründet und benutzte zunächst den Majlis Golfplatz, den ersten Meisterschaftsgrasplatz im Mittleren Osten. 1995 wurde er um den Wadi Golfplatz erweitert. Das Bild zeigt den Majlis-Platz und das Clubhaus in der Form von Beduinenzelten. Es wurde 2006 während des Dubai Desert Classic aufgenommen, aus dem schließlich Tiger Woods als Sieger hervorging. Der Wadi-Platz, unten im Bild, wurde im selben Jahr von Nick Faldo neu gestaltet und befindet sich daher gerade im Umbau.

Dubaï accueille le Dubai Desert Classic, qui fait désormais partie du Tour européen, à l'Emirates Golf Club. Le club a ouvert ses portes en 1988 avec le parcours Majlis, le premier Championship Golf Course tout-gazon de la région ; il a ensuite été agrandi en 1995, avec le parcours Wadi. Cette photo du parcours Majlis et du club-house, en forme de groupe de tentes de Bédouins, a été prise lors du Dubai Desert Classic de 2006, que remporta Tiger Woods. Le parcours Wadi, vers le bas de la photo, a été redessiné par Nick Faldo, aussi en 2006. On remarque les travaux en cours.

Дубай выступает в роли хозяина соревнования "Дубай Дезерт Классик", занимающего очень важное место в Европейском туре, в Эмиратском гольф-клубе. Этот клуб был открыт в 1988 году на площадке для гольфа "Маджлис" – первой во всем регионе травяной площадке для гольфа, и был расширен в 1995 году за счет площадки "Вади". Эта фотография площадки "Маджлис" и здания клуба в виде группы бедуинских палаток была сделана во время проведения "Дубай Дезерт Классик" в 2006 году, который в итоге выиграл Тайгер Вудс. Площадка "Вади" лежащая в направлении к нижней части фотографии, была переп-роектирована Ником Фалдо также в 2006 году, и ее можно видеть в процессе реконструкции.

عربي لقطة شاملة يظهر فيها عدد من المشاريع العقارية الفريدة التي أطلقتها شركة إعمار العقارية وهي مشاريع الروضة والينابيع وبحيرات وتلال الإمارات البادية إلى يمين الطريق المؤدي إلى مشروع الينابيع. وتظهر يسار الصورة جزر جميرا التي تنفذها شركة نخيل العقارية، وتلوح جزيرة نخلة جميرا في الأفق البعيد أعلى الصورة.

🇬🇧 Community living at Emaar's gated neighbourhoods, including The Meadows, The Springs, The Lakes and Emirates Hills to the right of Springs Drive, and Nakheel's Jumeirah Islands to the left. Note The Palm Jumeirah in the far distance.

🇩🇪 Das Bild zeigt die Wohngebiete von Emaar, zu denen die Communities The Meadows, The Springs, The Lakes und Emirates Hills rechts des Springs Drive gehören, sowie Jumeirah Islands von Nakheel links der Straße. In der Ferne ist The Palm Jumeirah zu sehen.

🇫🇷 Des communautés basées sur le principe du bon voisinage dans les quartiers protégés, parmi lesquels se trouvent les Meadows, les Springs, les Lakes et Emirates Hills à droite de Springs Drive, et Nakheel's Jumeirah Islands à gauche. Remarquez le Palm Jumeirah au loin.

🇷🇺 Община, живущая в закрытом районе Эмаар, включая Медоус, Спрингс, Лэйкс и Эмиратс Хиллс справа от Спрингс Драйв, и Джумейра Айлендс в Нахееле слева. Обратите внимание на видимую вдали Палм Джумейру.

بلغت ضخامة مساحة ميناء جبل علي الذي يضم ٧١ رصيفاً والذي يعد أكبر ميناء من صنع الإنسان في العالم، درجة تسمح بمشاهدته من الفضاء الخارجي. ويرتبط الميناء الذي يبعد ٣٥ كيلومتراً إلى الجنوب الغربي من مدينة دبي، بمنطقة حرة تجارية وصناعية توفر عدداً من المزايا الفريدة للشركات العاملة فيها ومن أبرزها حق تملك مشاريعها بنسبة ١٠٠ في المائة والإعفاء التام من شتى أنواع الضرائب.

The 71-berth Jebel Ali Port, the world's largest man-made harbour, some 35 kilometres south-west of Dubai, is so large that it's visible from space. Jebel Ali has its own free zone, a commercial and industrial area which provides companies with a range of benefits that include 100-per-cent ownership in a tax-free environment.

Le port de Jebel Ali, le port artificiel le plus grand du monde, avec ses 71 amarrages, situé à 35 kilomètres au sud-ouest de Dubaï, est tellement grand qu'il est visible de l'espace. Jebel Ali a sa propre zone franche, une zone industrielle et commerciale, qui apporte aux sociétés une série d'avantages, y compris l'actionnariat à cent pour cent pour les expatriés dans un environnement sans impôt.

Der größte künstliche Hafen der Welt, Jebel Ali, 35 Kilometer südwestlich von Dubai gelegen, ist mit seinen 71 Anlegeplätzen so groß, dass er aus dem Weltraum sichtbar ist. Er verfügt über eine Freihandelszone mit Geschäfts- und Industriebereich. Die hier angesiedelten Unternehmen genießen viele Vorteile, wie beispielsweise vollständiges Eigentumsrecht und Steuerfreiheit.

Оснащенный 71 причалом Джебел Али Порт – самый большой в мире искусственный порт, расположенный примерно в 35 километрах к юго-западу от Дубая, – настолько огромен, что виден даже из космоса. У Джебел Али есть своя собственная свободная зона-торгово-промышленная территория, которая предоставляет кампаниям целый ряд льгот, в том числе стопроцентное право собственности в свободной от налогов окружающей среде.

تتناقض سكينة الصحراء وجمالها تماماً مع صخب وضجيج مدينة دبي المزدهرة، التي لا تبعد عنها سوى مقدار نصف الساعة بالسيارة. وقد كان الانتقال بين أنحاء دولة الإمارات العربية المتحدة على ظهور الجمال حتى وقت غير بعيد، بات من الممكن بلوغ حتى مناطق الدولة النائية بالسيارات، بفضل شبكة الطرق الممتازة التي تخترق الصحارى والجبال والمدن وتصل إلى كل مكان.

🇬🇧 In total contrast to the excitement and vibrancy of the city, the stillness and beauty of the desert can be experienced just a half-hour's drive away from Dubai. Until relatively recently, many parts of the United Arab Emirates could only be reached by camel. Now even remote areas have been made accessible by tarmac roads that slice through the desert and mountains.

🇩🇪 Die Ruhe und Schönheit der Wüste bilden einen starken Kontrast zum aufregenden und pulsierenden Leben der Großstadt und sind doch nur dreißig Autominuten entfernt. Bis vor Kurzem waren weite Teile der Vereinigten Arabischen Emirate nur per Dromedar zu erreichen, aber inzwischen führen Asphaltpisten, die die Wüste und Berge durchschneiden, sogar bis in die entferntesten Winkel.

🇫🇷 En contraste absolu avec l'excitation et l'agitation de la ville, le calme et la beauté du désert peuvent être ressentis à moins d'une demi-heure de Dubaï en voiture. Jusqu'à il n'y a pas si longtemps on ne pouvait rejoindre les quatre coins des Émirats qu'à dos de chameau. Aujourd'hui, on peut accéder, même aux endroits les plus éloignés, par des routes goudronnées qui traversent le désert et les montagnes.

🇷🇺 На полном контрасте с возбуждением и вибрациями городской жизни всего лишь через полчаса езды на автомобиле из Дубая можно почувствовать безмолвие и красоту пустыни. Относительно до недавнего времени многие районы ОАЭ можно было достичь только на верблюдах. Теперь даже удаленные территории стали доступны благодаря гудронированным дорогам, которые проходят через пустыню и горы.

بغض النظر عن التطورات المتلاحقة التي تشهدها المدينة، تحافظ الصحراء على ديمومتها السرمدية. غير أنه في الوقت الذي كانت فيه الصحراء في الماضي مقر قبائل البدو الرحل، باتت تجتذب اليوم نوعاً جديداً من الناس الذين يقومون برحلات سفاري صحراوية ممتعة لمدة يوم واحد. ويتمتع المشاركون في مثل تلك الرحلات بجمال الصحراء وركوب الجمال والتزلج فوق كثبان الرمال. كما يستطيعون أحياناً مشاهدة سباقات الهجن الأصيلة واستحضار صور الماضي حين كانت قوافل الجمال تسير في غياهب الصحراء.

Whatever exciting developments may be under way in the city, the desert has a permanence of its own. While the nomadic Bedu of yesteryear have settled for a sedentary life, the silence and beauty of the desert now draws the resident and visitor for day-long excursions in the dunefields. A ride on a camel is unforgettable; a smooth experience where the camel appears to glide over the sand. Very occasionally, racing camels may be seen in the desert, being exercised by their trainers and conjuring up romantic images of the nomadic Bedu and their camel caravans of times past.

Unabhängig von den aufregenden Entwicklungen der Stadt besitzt die Wüste ihre ureigene Beständigkeit. Während die Bedu (Nomaden) von einst sich inzwischen für ein sesshaftes Leben entschieden haben, ziehen die Ruhe und die Schönheit der Wüste jetzt Anwohner und Besucher gleichermaßen an, um Tagesausflüge in die Dünenfelder zu unternehmen. Ein Ritt auf einem Dromedar ist eine unvergessliche Erfahrung: Sanft gleiten die Wüstenschiffe über den Sand. Ab und zu sind Renndromedare in der Wüste zu sehen, die von ihren Betreuern trainiert werden: ein romantisches Bild, das an die vergangenen Zeiten der Nomaden und Karawanen erinnert.

Malgré toutes les évolutions les plus passionnantes en ville, le désert conserve sa propre perennité. Alors que les Bédouins nomades d'antan se sont sédentarisés, le silence et la beauté du désert attirent toujours les résidents et les visiteurs, pour des excursions dans les dunes. Une promenade à dos de chameau est inoubliable – une expérience étonnamment paisible où l'on dirait que le chameau glisse sur le sable. On voit parfois des chameaux de course dans le désert avec leurs entraîneurs, évoquant des images romantiques des Bédouins nomades d'antan avec leurs caravanes de chameaux.

Какие бы волнующие процессы не происходили в городе, пустыня все равно демонстрирует свою собственную неизменность. Несмотря на то, что кочевники-бедуины в недавнем прошлом перешли к оседлой жизни, тишина и красота пустыни теперь привлекают местного жителя и гостя совершить однодневные экскурсии в дюны. Езда верхом на верблюде незабываема; приятное впечатление возникает в тот момент, когда начинает казаться, что верблюд плавно плывет над песками. Очень редко можно видеть в пустыне бегущих верблюдов, которых тренируют их погонщики и которые вызывают в воображении романтические образы кочевников-бедуинов и их верблюжьих караванов в прошедшие времена.

عربي تعبر رحلات السفاري الصحراوية المتجهة إلى قرية حتّا التي تبعد نحو ١٠٠ كيلومتر عن دبي، كثباناً ضخمة ومرتفعة من الرمال الحمراء الناعمة قبل أن تصل إلى سلسلة جبال الحجر المهيبة. وتوفر مثل هذه الرحلات فرصة مثالية للذين لا يمتلكون سيارات دفع رباعي، للتمتع بجمال الصحراء وطبيعتها الفريدة.

On the road to Hatta, an oasis some 100 kilometres from Dubai, you'll pass towering dunes of red sand before encountering the stark landscape of the Hajar Mountains. Desert safaris, offered by commercial operators, are ideal for those without a 4x4 who are keen to explore the outdoor wilderness.

Sur la route d'Hatta, une oasis à environ 100 kilomètres de Dubaï, vous traverserez d'imposantes dunes de sable rouge, puis vous vous trouverez face au paysage aride des montagnes du Hajar. Des safaris dans le désert, proposés par des opérateurs commerciaux sont idéals pour ceux qui n'ont pas de 4x4 mais qui veulent explorer la nature.

Die Straße nach Hatta, einer Oase in 100 Kilometer Entfernung von Dubai, führt vorbei an hohen Dünen aus rotem Sand, bevor die kahle Landschaft der Hajar-Berge erreicht wird. Reiseveranstalter haben Wüstensafaris im Programm, die auch denen, die über keinen eigenen Geländewagen verfügen, die Möglichkeit bieten, die Wüste zu erforschen.

По дороге в Хатту – оазис, лежащий приблизительно в 100 километрах от Дубая, – вы сначала пройдете через возвышающиеся дюны из красного песка, а затем вступите на твердый ландшафт Хаджарских гор. Пустынные сафари, предлагаемые коммерческими операторами, идеально подходят для тех без "4x4", кто стремится исследовать дикую природу под открытым небом.

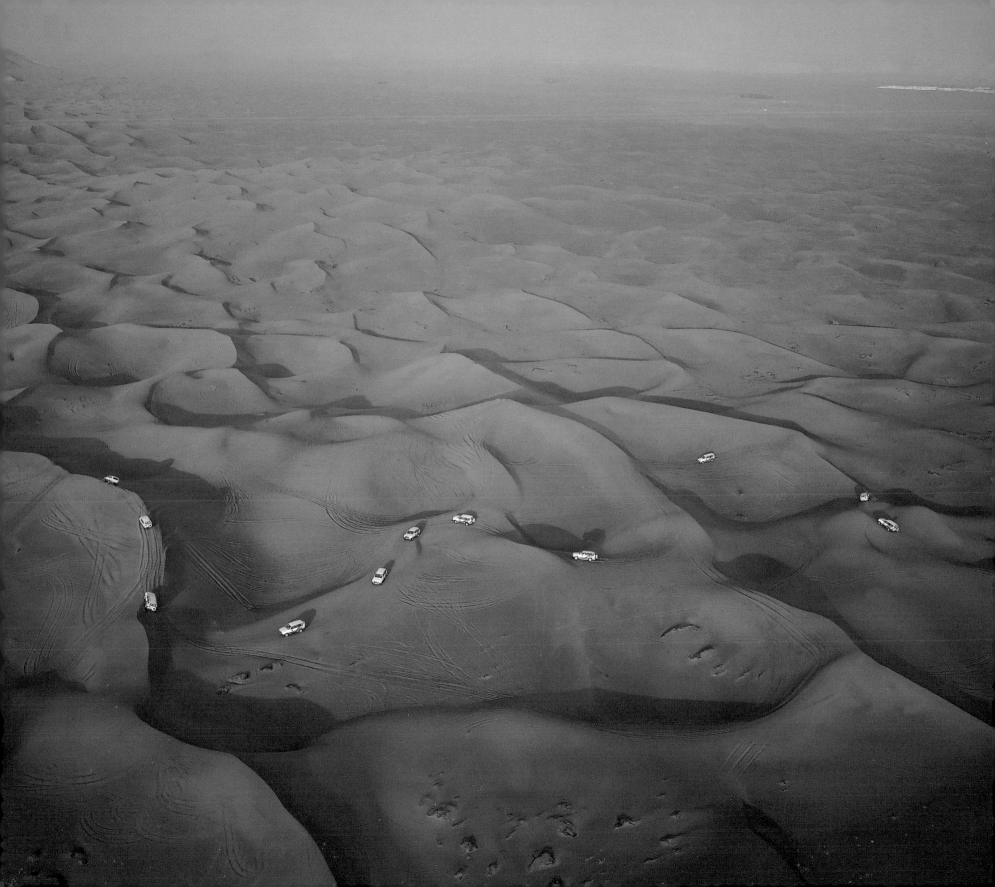

عربي كانت الحياة في الصحارى مختلفة قبل اكتشاف النفط، حيث كان يرتادها البدو الرحل في قوافل كبيرة من الجمال التي تنقلهم وأفراد أسرهم ومتاعهم بين المناطق التي يتوفر فيها الكلأ لمواشيهم. غير أن الثروة النفطية سمحت للحكومة بتوطين البدو في قرى ثابتة مثل هذه القرية الظاهرة في الصورة والتي يتوسطها مسجد.

🇬🇧 Before the discovery of oil, life was very different for the Bedouin who roamed the hot desert with their camel herds. With the discovery of oil and its vast revenues, the nomads were encouraged to settle, and modern villages were constructed for them, as in the settlement pictured, which encircles the community's mosque.

🇫🇷 La vie avant la découverte du pétrole était très différente pour les Bédouins qui parcouraient le désert brûlant avec leurs troupeaux de chameaux. À la suite de la découverte du pétrole et ses énormes revenus, on a encouragé les nomades à se sédentariser ; on leur a construit des villages modernes, comme l'ensemble résidentiel de la photo qui encercle la mosquée de la communauté.

🇩🇪 Vor der Entdeckung des Erdöls war das Leben für die Beduinen, die mit ihren Herden durch die heiße Wüste zogen, ganz anders als heute. Die Entdeckung des schwarzen Goldes und die damit verbundenen Einnahmen führten dazu, dass sie sesshaft wurden. Moderne Siedlungen, wie die hier gezeigte mit der Moschee in der Mitte, wurden für sie gebaut.

🇷🇺 До открытия нефти для бедуинов, которые странствовали по жарким пустыням со стадами своих верблюдов, жизнь была совсем другой. С обнаружением нефти и получением от нее очень больших доходов кочевников убедили перейти к оседлому образу жизни, и для них были построены современные деревни, наподобие показанного на фотографии поселения, которое окружает общинную мечеть.

شكلت الجمال المحور الرئيسي لنمط حياة البدو في الصحراء، حيث كانت توفر لهم وسيلة المواصلات الوحيدة القادرة على عبور الصحراء، ومصدراً للحليب واللحوم والصوف والماء أحياناً خلال السفر، إضافة إلى كونها أداة للترفيه من خلال سباقات الهجن. وكان البدو يستخدمون جلود الجمال وعظامها في صنع الملابس والحقائب والأدوات المنزلية.

Camels have been the mainstay of traditional Arab life for centuries. Regarded as God's gift to the Bedouin, these ships of the desert are exceptionally suited to their harsh environment. Prior to the advent of the faster, but less efficient motor vehicle, they provided a means of transport, sport in the form of camel racing and sustenance from their milk and meat. Nothing was wasted. If a camel was slaughtered to celebrate a wedding or other special occasion, their hides, bones and hair were used to make bags, utensils and garments.

Les chameaux ont été le pilier de la vie arabe traditionnelle pendant des siècles. Considérés comme cadeaux de Dieu aux Bédouins, ces « vaisseaux » du désert sont exceptionnellement bien adaptés à leur rude environnement. Avant l'arrivée des véhicules à moteur, qui sont certes plus rapides, mais moins efficaces, les chameaux fournissaient un moyen de transport, du sport sous la forme de courses de chameaux, et de la nourriture de par leur lait et leur viande. Rien n'était gaspillé. Lorsqu'un chameau était sacrifié pour fêter un mariage ou quelque autre évènement spécial, sa peau, ses os et ses poils étaient utilisés pour fabriquer des sacs, des outils et des vêtements.

Die Dromedare waren jahrhundertelang die Hauptstütze der traditionellen Wirtschaft Arabiens. Sie passen sich der rauen Umgebung besonders gut an und gelten als Gottes Geschenk an die Beduinen. Vor der Einführung der schnelleren, aber weniger effizienten Motorfahrzeuge, dienten sie als Transportmittel, Sport- und Nutztiere, die Milch- und Fleisch lieferten. Nichts wurde verschwendet; ein anlässlich einer Hochzeit oder einer anderen besonderen Gelegenheit geschlachtetes Dromedar steuerte seine Haut, Knochen und Haare zur Herstellung von Taschen, Kleidung und Gebrauchsgegenständen bei.

В течение столетий верблюды были основой традиционной жизни арабов. Рассматриваемые в качестве подарка Бога бедуинам, эти корабли пустыни исключительно приспособлены к суровым условиям своего существования. До появления более быстрого, но менее эффективного автомобиля, они были средством транспорта, участниками спортивных состязаний в форме верблюжьих гонок и средством к существованию из-за их молока и мяса. Ничто не выбрасывалось. Если верблюда убивали, чтобы отпраздновать свадьбу или другое событие, его шкура, кости и шерсть использовались для изготовления мешков, утвари и одежды.

تتراوح أشكال وألوان كثبان الرمال بين السمني الفاتح قرب السواحل والأحمر الداكن في باطن الصحراء، حيث تحف بها تجمعات من الصخور وسهول من الحصى من مختلف الأحجام. وتتغير أحجام كثبان الرمال بين عشية وضحاها تبعاً لمدى قوة واتجاه هبوب الرياح وحجم حبات الرمل التي تتألف منها. وهكذا نجد أن بعض الكثبان ليست سوى تموجات من الرمال فوق سطح الأرض، بينما نجد كثباناً عملاقة يتجاوز ارتفاع الواحد منها ١٠٠ متر. وتوفر بعض الكثبان ذات السفوح الحادة، التحديات الكبرى التي يبحث عنها عشاق قيادة سيارات الدفع الرباعي في الصحراء.

The dunefields are made up of many different landscapes, their colours varying from pale cream near the sea to deep red inland, dotted with outcrops of rock and gravel plains of varying sizes throughout. The height and form of the dunes changes too, depending on the prevailing wind and the size and shape of the individual grains of sand, so that some are mere gentle undulations while others tower 100 metres or more, their knife-edge crests providing the perfect challenge for quad-bikers and off-road drivers in their sturdy 4x4s.

Die Dünenfelder bestehen aus vielen unterschiedlichen Landschaften in mehreren Farben, von weißgelb in Küstennähe bis dunkelrot im Landesinnern, durchsetzt von Felsen und Kiesplateaus unterschiedlicher Größe. Auch die Höhe und Form der Dünen verändern sich ständig. Unterschiedliche Stärke und Richtung des Windes sowie die Größe und Form der einzelnen Sandkörner können zu sanften Wellenlandschaften oder über 100 Meter hohen Sandklippen führen. Die steilen Hänge dieser Klippen stellen eine wunderbare Herausforderung für Quad- und Geländewagenfahrer dar.

Les champs de dunes sont composés de nombreux paysages dont les couleurs changent d'un crème pâle près de la mer à un rouge foncé à l'intérieur des terres, parsemés de roches saillantes et de plaines de gravier. La hauteur et la forme des dunes changent aussi en fonction des vents dominants, de la taille et de la forme des grains de sable formant des dunes qui parfois ne seront que de petites ondulations douces alors que d'autres fois, elles seront hautes de 100 mètres ou plus, leurs crêtes effilées fournissant le défi parfait pour les quadistes et les conducteurs de véhicules tout terrain dans leurs robustes 4x4.

Дюны включают в себя много различных ландшафтов, причем их цвета варьируются от бледно-кремового около моря до темно-красного внутри материка; они повсюду усеяны скальными выходами и площадками гравия разных размеров. Высота и форма дюн также меняется, что зависит от действия господствующего ветра и размерpjd и формы отдельных песчинок. Поэтому некоторые из дюн представляют собой лишь простые неровные поверхности, тогда как другие возвышаются на 100 метров и больше, причем их лезвиеобразные гребни бросают весьма серьезный вызов квадбайкерам и водителям по бездорожью на их прочных "4x4".

عربى تنتشر الجبال في صحارى دولة الإمارات العربية المتحدة، لتفاجىء الزائرين بأن طبيعة الدولة لا تقتصر على الصحراء والبحر فحسب وإنما تضم الجبال أيضاً. وترتفع قمم تلك الجبال التي تعد سلسلة جبال الحجر قاسمها المشترك، لتمنح الأفق مشهداً مهيباً لقمم حادة جرداء. وتضم الوديان التي تتخلل تلك الجبال، العديد من القرى التي لا تزال مأهولة حتى اليوم، حيث يعتمد سكانها على الزراعة وتربية المواشي، بفضل توفر المياه من الأمطار والينابيع.

Jebels (mountains) taper throughout the UAE's interior, offering stark evidence of the power of the earth's shifting tectonic plates and, for visitors who often expect nothing but flat desert, the UAE's varied topography comes as something of a surprise. The mountain ridges are barren but beautiful, with picturesque villages deep in the valleys. In the *wadis*, gouged out by winter rains, trees maintain a precarious hold, while high above, the barren crests bake in the sun.

Des *jebels* (montagnes) surgissent partout à l'intérieur des Émirats, témoignage de la brutale puissance du déplacement des plaques tectoniques ; les visiteurs, qui ne s'attendent généralement qu'à du désert plat, sont souvent surpris par la topographie variée des Émirats. Les chaînes de montagne sont arides mais magnifiques, avec leurs villages pittoresques au fond des vallées. Dans les *wadis*, creusés par les pluies de l'hiver, des arbres s'accrochent de façon précaire, alors que, loin au-dessus d'eux, les crêtes arides brûlent sous le soleil.

Das Landesinnere der VAE ist durchsetzt von *Jebels* (Bergen), Zeugen der Kraft der sich verschiebenden tektonischen Erdplatten. Der Besucher, der häufig nichts als flache Wüste erwartet, ist von der vielfältigen Topographie der Emirate oft überrascht. Die Bergketten sind karg, aber besitzen eine eigene Schönheit, und in den Tälern finden sich malerische Dörfer. In den von den Winterregen ausgehöhlten *Wadis* krallen sich Bäume an die Erde, während hoch oben die Kämme in der Sonne dörren.

Джебелс (горы) суживаются на всем протяжении внутренних районов ОАЭ, давая тем самым яркое свидетельство силы перемещения тектонических пластов земли, а для гостей, которые ожидают увидеть только однообразную пустыню, разнообразная топография ОАЭ становится чем-то вроде сюрприза. Горные хребты бесплодны, но красивы, вместе с живописными деревнями в глубине долин. В вади, выдолбленных зимними дождями, деревья не имеют надежного убежища, тогда как высоко над ними бесплодные хребты купаются в лучах солнца.

تبعد قرية حتا الجبلية التابعة لإمارة دبي، ٩٠ دقيقة بالسيارة عن مدينة دبي، ويعتقد أنها من أقدم المناطق التي قطنها الإنسان في دولة الإمارات العربية المتحدة. وتشير الآثار التي تم اكتشافها إلى أن عمر القرية يعود إلى ثلاثة آلاف عام مضت. ويحرس القرية برجان مستديران بينما ترويها شبكة رائعة من الأفلاج. وتوفر القرية التراثية التي تمت إقامتها في حتّا، لمحة وافية عن نمط الحياة الذي كان سائداً في الماضي، حيث تم تأهيل المنازل القديمة التي تم بناؤها باستخدام سعف النخيل والطين.

This roundabout (with the Hatta Fort Hotel in the background) marks the main entrance to Hatta, some 90 minutes away from the city towards the east coast of the peninsula, and part of the Emirate of Dubai. Hatta is thought to be one of the oldest inhabited places in the emirate, with archaeological evidence dating back some 3,000 years. The town is guarded by two round watchtowers and boasts fascinating *falaj* (irrigation) systems. Hatta's Heritage Village offers a glimpse into the lives of the people of ancient Arabia, with fully restored mud houses and palm-tree products that were used on a daily basis, made from palm fronds and from the dates they produced.

Hatta, un village à 90 minutes de la ville et qui appartient à l'Émirat de Dubaï, est situé à l'intérieur des terres en direction de la côte est de la péninsule. On estime que c'est le plus ancien emplacement habité de l'Émirat, avec des témoignages archéologiques qui remontent à quelque 3 000 années. Le village est protégé par deux tours de guet et possède des systèmes fascinants de *falaj* (irrigation). Le village traditionnel de Hatta permet d'avoir un aperçu de la vie des peuples de l'ancienne Arabie. On y trouve des maisons de terre qui ont été totalement restaurées, des produits issus du palmier qui étaient utilisés au quotidien, et qui étaient fabriqués avec des feuilles de palmiers ou des dattes.

Hatta liegt etwa 90 Minuten von der Stadt Dubai entfernt im Landesinnern, in Richtung Ostküste der Halbinsel. Der Ort gilt als eine der ältesten Siedlungen des Emirats. Hier wurden archäologische Funde gemacht, die etwa 3.000 Jahre alt sind. Die Stadt wird von zwei Wachtürmen beschützt und verfügt über faszinierende *Falaj*, oder Bewässerungssysteme. Das örtliche Museumsdorf ermöglicht einen Einblick in das Leben der Bevölkerung des Alten Arabiens, mit vollständig renovierten Lehmhütten und Alltagsprodukten, die aus den Blättern und Früchten der Dattelpalme gewonnen wurden.

Хатта – это город примерно в 90 минутах езды от Дубая и часть Дубайского эмирата, лежащий внутри материка по направлению к восточному побережью полуострова. Он считается одним из древнейших обитаемых мест в эмирате – согласно археологическим данным, ему уже около 3000 лет. Город охраняется двумя круглыми наблюдательными башнями и гордится своей приводящей в восторг ирригационной системой *фаладж*. "Деревня исторического наследия" в Хатте позволяет бросить взгляд на жизнь людей в древней Аравии, ознакомиться с полностью восстановленными сырцовыми домами и продуктами, произведенными из листьев и плодов пальмовых деревьев, которые использовались в те давние времена в повседневной жизни.